PSYCHIATRIC EXAMINATION
IN CLINICAL PRACTICE

Psychiatric Examination
in Clinical Practice

J. P. LEFF BSc, MD,
MRCP, FRCPsych
Director
MRC Social and Community Psychiatry Unit
Institute of Psychiatry
De Crespigny Park, London

A. D. ISAACS FRCP, FRCPsych
Consultant Psychiatrist
Bethlem Royal and Maudsley Hospitals
Denmark Hill, London

THIRD EDITION

Oxford

BLACKWELL SCIENTIFIC PUBLICATIONS

London Edinburgh Boston

Melbourne Paris Berlin Vienna

First published 1978
Reprinted 1979
Second Edition 1981
Reprinted 1983, 1986
Third Edition 1990

Set by DP Photosetting,
Aylesbury, Bucks
Printed and bound in Great Britain
by Billings and Sons Ltd, Worcester

DISTRIBUTORS

Marston Book Services Ltd
PO Box 87
Oxford OX2 0DT
(*Orders*: Tel. 0865 791155
         Fax: 0865 791927
         Telex: 837515)

USA
Year Book Medical Publishers
200 North LaSalle Street
Chicago, Illinois 60601
(*Orders*: Tel: (312) 726-9733)

Canada
The C.V. Mosby Company
5240 Finch Avenue East
Scarborough, Ontario
(*Orders*: Tel: (416) 298-1588)

Australia
Blackwell Scientific Publications
(Australia) Pty Ltd
54 University Street
Carlton, Victoria 3053
(*Orders*: Tel: (03) 347-0300)

British Library Cataloguing in
Publication Data

Leff, J. P. (Julian Paul)
  Psychiatric examination in
  clinical practice.—3rd ed.
  1. Man. Mental disorders. Diagnosis
  I. Title   II. Isaacs, A. D.
  616.89075

  ISBN 0–632–02878–5

Contents

CHAPTER ONE

Introduction

Diagnosis in medicine used to rest entirely on the skills of taking a detailed history and conducting a careful physical examination of the patient. These traditional skills have been somewhat eroded by the development of pathological investigations, such as radiography and biochemical tests. However, these developments in scientific medicine have left psychiatry virtually untouched. Certain pathological investigations are of use in identifying organic cerebral conditions, such as temporal lobe dysfunction and cortical atrophy, but they contribute nothing to the diagnosis of the functional psychoses and neurotic conditions. When dealing with these illnesses, the psychiatrist is entirely reliant on his skill in taking a history and conducting an examination of the patient's mental state. Both these activities are aimed at the eventual formulation of a diagnosis. Therefore, the diagnostic significance of the possible responses to questions about the history or the mental state should be fully appreciated by the psychiatrist. If his awareness of this becomes dulled by time and habit, it is all too easy for the diagnostic interview to become an empty ritual instead of a piece of careful detective work.

The pressure of a busy clinic compels most psychiatrists to cut corners in their interviews, but this should be done in a logical way; only to the extent of omitting probes for information which is not going to contribute to a diagnosis. Furthermore, the psychiatrist should always be aware of what the full interview comprises. The schemata that have been put forward in this book for inquiring into the history and the mental state have been constructed with an eventual formulation of a diagnosis in mind. To this aim, attempts have been made to exclude items which do not help in the diagnostic process.

A strong emphasis has been placed on the phenomena of mental illness, that is, those aspects of the subject's speech and behaviour which can be directly observed. No attempt has been made here to deal with more inferential material, such as the dynamics of the patient's relationship with his parents or with the psychiatrist. The reader is advised to consult other books for this extremely important material.

The phenomena of mental illness are comparable to abnormal heart sounds in cardiac disease or a palpable liver in hepatic conditions. There is an important difference, however, in that arguments about the quality and clinical significance of abnormal heart sounds can be resolved by cardiac catheterisation or direct observation during heart surgery. There are no objective means of resolving disagreements about the definition of psychiatric symptoms and their clinical significance. The value of symptoms is that they lead to a diagnosis so that ultimately it is a matter of establishing the validity of diagnostic categories and processes. Until we have some pathological test for the presence of, say, schizophrenia that is independent of symptoms, we cannot state with assurance that symptom X is diagnostic of schizophrenia. All we can say is that when a patient exhibits symptom X, psychiatrist Y will make a diagnosis of schizophrenia.

If psychiatrist Y operates an idiosyncratic system of diagnosis, he will find it difficult to communicate with other psychiatrists about patients and illnesses. Fortunately, within any one country there is usually fairly good agreement between psychiatrists about diagnostic categories, although this is invariably worse for personality disorders than for the functional psychoses. There is also good agreement internationally on a narrow definition of schizophrenia. If one or more of Schneider's (1957) first rank symptoms are present, nearly every psychiatrist from a wide variety of countries will make a diagnosis of schizophrenia (World Health Organisation 1973). The virtually universal adoption of Schneider's first rank symptoms as criteria for the presence of schizophrenia is due in part to the clarity of most of his definitions and in part to the fact that they appear to be applicable in any culture. However, outside the core group of patients with first rank symptoms, there is considerable disagreement among an international sample of psychiatrists over the diagnosis of the functional psychoses, and no way of deciding who is right. It is of relevance to this distinction between schizophrenia with and without first rank symptoms, that the incidence of the former is relatively uniform across cultures, whereas the latter shows significant variations in incidence (Sartorius *et al* 1986).

In the current state of ignorance about the validity of diagnostic categories, it is essential that every psychiatrist be prepared to list the symptoms on which he bases his diagnoses, and furthermore that he is able to give a precise definition of each symptom. In this book we have inevitably introduced our own system of diagnosis, as it is impossible to teach the elucidation of symptoms without referring to their diagnostic significance. Our bias needs to be assessed in the light of our being in the mainstream of British psychiatric practice. Its effect should be alleviated by the fact that we have given as precise a definition as possible of each symptom. Thus a reader operating a diagnostic system that differs from ours could still benefit from the instruction given here on the eliciting of signs and symptoms provided that his system is based on these phenomena.

Disagreement among psychiatrists is not confined to diagnostic categories but also extends to the definition of symptoms. Again there is no way of externally validating symptoms, only a consensus of agreement. In this situation the only objective criterion that can be applied to such definitions is whether they satisfy the requirements of an ideal system of categorisation, namely that the categories be mutually exclusive and collectively exhaustive. As applied to symptoms this means that the definitions should not overlap with each other and should cover the whole range of morbid phenomena in psychiatry. We have been closely guided by these aims in preparing this book. We have been greatly helped in this task by our experience with the Present State Examination

(Wing *et al* 1974). This is a semi-structured clinical interview which was constructed as a research tool. Each symptom inquired about has a precisely formulated definition, which has to be mastered before the interview can be properly conducted. Both of us are familiar with the Present State Examination and one of us (JL) has been teaching its use regularly for some years to people wishing to use it in research. This teaching experience has been of great value in identifying common confusions between certain symptoms, for example delusions of control and compulsions. Special emphasis has consequently been placed on clarifying such confusions here.

Another gain from teaching the Present State Examination has been the realisation that non-verbal signs, such as facial expression and bodily posture are relatively neglected in psychiatric training. There seems to be a general assumption that these aspects of patients' mental state are recognised instinctively and hence do not need to be formally taught. However, when trainees are asked to verbalise about non-verbal signs, they are almost invariably at a loss. An attempt has been made to redress this neglect since a great deal of diagnostic importance can be learned about the patient before he speaks a word. These matters are dealt with in Chapter Four. Furthermore, some patients cannot communicate verbally because of muteness, or some other problem, and non-verbal cues are of the greatest importance in these cases. The difficulties presented by such patients are discussed in Chapter Nine.

In this book we have focused on the adult patient, but children make up an increasing proportion of psychiatric practice and differ in a number of important respects from adult patients. Not only are different skills required in the examination of children, but many of the conditions exhibited by adults are not seen in children. For these reasons Chapter Ten is devoted to the psychiatric examination of children including an assessment of a child suspected of having been sexually abused.

In the final chapter we discuss the ways in which the material collected during the clinical interview may be organised for the purposes both of making a diagnosis and of presenting the case to colleagues.

Many of the issues touched on in this book are discussed at length in the psychiatric literature. We have decided, however, not to clutter the text with innumerable references nor to append an extensive bibliography as we feel this would detract from our aim to produce a practical handbook.

REFERENCES

SARTORIUS, N., JABLENSKY, A., KORTEN, G., ERNBERG, G., ANKER, M., COOPER, J. E. & DAY, R. (1986) Early manifestations and first-contact incidence of schizophrenia in different cultures. *Psychological Medicine*, **16**, 909–28.

SCHNEIDER, K. (1957) Primäre und sekundäre Symptome bei der Schizophrenie. *Fortschritte der Neurologie und Psychiatrie*, **25**, 487–90.
A translation of this paper is included in:

HIRSCH, S. R. & SHEPHERD, M. (Eds.) (1974) *Themes and Variations in European Psychiatry: An Anthology*. Bristol: John Wright and Sons.

WING, J. K., COOPER, J. E. & SARTORIUS, N. (1974) *The Measurement and Classification of Psychiatric Symptoms*. Cambridge University Press, London.

WORLD HEALTH ORGANISATION (1973) *The International Pilot Study of Schizophrenia*. Vol. 1. World Health Organisation, Geneva.

History-taking:
The Presenting Problem

INTRODUCTION

A distinguished cardiologist has been quoted as saying that he could teach auscultation in a matter of months but the ability to take a complete history took years to acquire. With advances in medical technology the importance of the history in clinical practice generally has diminished, often to the point of being a largely meaningless superficial ritual. In psychiatry it is essential that the history should be seen as by far the most important aspect of the psychiatric interview. Its importance is such that every trainee psychiatrist should make a commitment at the outset to achieve high and consistent standards of history-taking even though, as indicated by the cardiologist, years of experience may be needed to become fully competent.

Why should such emphasis be placed on the importance of history-taking in psychiatry? Firstly, the information obtained is an indispensible element in the diagnostic process. Secondly, but perhaps of equal importance, while obtaining a narrative account of the patient's problems and background, the opportunity arises to establish a proper working relationship or rapport with the patient. If the patient can sense in the examiner qualities of genuineness, an ability to understand his problems and a warm friendly but non-possessive manner, a trusting relationship can develop in which far more will emerge than when the right sort of relationship is not established. It is at the history stage of the examination that the opportunity arises to gain the patient's confidence in this way and form a sound basis for the clinical interview. The ability to establish a good relationship with patients is something that may take time to acquire but becomes easier with increasing experience and confidence. As an objective, however, it is of paramount importance.

As a source of information the history will only be of value if, in its final form, it gives a systematic account of the patient, and this will only be achieved if a consistent approach or scheme is used *each* time an examination is carried out. While the basic framework for the history should always be the same, the way in which the information is obtained will vary according to the clinical circumstances. In practice, the history rarely emerges in an orderly chronological sequence, but by making rough notes if necessary, the examiner can later put the information together in a coherent way in accordance with the particular scheme he* has adopted. This chapter, and the one that follows, will suggest a comprehensive scheme, but one problem often is 'where to start'.

Since flexibility of technique is always necessary there can be no standard way to begin the history, but as a general rule, even when an informant is available, the *patient should be seen first* and will usually prefer to talk about his immediate worries and problems, in which case the history would start with an account of the present illness. There are occasions, however, when a patient will deny any difficulties. Rather than draw the interview to a premature close in such circumstances, it would be wise to undertake a systematic account of the patient's background. While doing so, significant clues may then emerge as to the real nature of his problem, which can then be clarified in the usual way.

In taking the *history of the present condition,* it is extremely useful to try to record the main problems in the patient's own words rather than paraphrase his account using technical terms the appropriateness of which can often be disputed. The patient might find it difficult at the beginning of the interview to discuss his main

---

* For the sake of brevity 'he' will be used for 'he or she' throughout the book.

problems, and a short period of 'neutral' conversation will be helpful before trying to focus the patient's attention on his symptoms. Some patients will spontaneously discuss their worries but in most cases an explanatory question will be needed, eg 'What do you feel is your main problem?'; 'What's worrying you?'; 'Why did you go to the doctor?'; 'Perhaps you could tell me about your difficulties', and so on. A detailed account of the present problem should then follow and wherever possible this should include the following information:

1 When did the illness *start*? This might be established by asking the patient when he feels he was last entirely well or when he first sought medical or other help.

2 Was there anything that *precipitated* the illness? Certain *life events* are known to unmask some psychiatric illnesses. Symptoms might develop a short while after a bereavement, or getting the sack from work or moving house, and special inquiry would be needed to determine whether such circumstances had existed at the time the illness began. *Physical* factors can also precipitate certain conditions and the possibility will need careful exploration in the history, eg a previously well-adjusted healthy woman of 25 suddenly developed bouts of tearfulness, and fear of enclosed places. Questioning revealed that shortly before the onset, she had started a new oral contraceptive drug which was later confirmed as the sole cause of her disability. In the case of an elderly patient presenting with confusional symptoms, such as visual hallucinations, disorientation or a lowered level of consciousness, the history may reveal the underlying cause. Thus there might be a history of a recent pyrexial illness, a head injury, operation, or habitual heavy drinking with a recent reduction in the amount of alcohol taken. A depressed patient might be found to have recently had influenza and a schizophrenic patient to have stopped taking his maintenance medication. The identification of such factors is not only important in reaching a diagnosis but may help with the management of the patient's condition as well as providing some indication of how the illness might be prevented in the future.

3 How did the condition *develop*? The mode of onset of a

9

psychiatric illness can give important clues as to the likely *cause*. Thus a lady of 76 was found wandering in the street, unable to recall her address, give her correct age, name the year or month or have any awareness of her surroundings. A provisional diagnosis of advanced dementia was made until it later transpired that until two days before she was found, she had been an alert, active independent person, with a remarkably good memory for her age. She had knocked her head just before the troubles started. This history led to full neurological investigation and a diagnosis of subdural haematoma.

The mode of onset might also have implications for *prognosis*; an illness that develops slowly and insidiously is likely to have a less favourable prognosis than one in which there is a sudden, clearcut time of onset.

4   What is the *severity* of the illness? The extent to which the patient suffers distress will be the most important guide to the seriousness of the condition. Its social effects will also reflect the severity and an inquiry about them often proves a useful way of confirming the patient's subjective experiences. These will be revealed by considering changes in the patient's habitual life pattern such as work or leisure activities. For example, a patient with a mild phobic disorder might feel some discomfort while travelling by underground but when severe he will avoid the situation entirely. As a rule increasing severity causes increasing disruption of everyday life.

A useful way of assessing disability is to consider a typical day in the patient's life (Abrahamson 1974) and this can be contrasted with a comparable day prior to the onset of the illness. This might also reveal the presence of *physical* symptoms which always need to be considered. Direct questions are usually required for their clarification. These should include an inquiry about changes in appetite, body weight, bowel habits, sleep pattern and sexual behaviour. Thus, loss of appetite with an accompanying loss of body weight is a common physical feature of *depressive illness* and can also be a guide to its severity. Associated features might be a reduction in sexual drive and interest, leading to impotence in men or frigidity in women. Constipation or some general concern about bowel function are also common physical features as well as sleep disturbance. Early morning waking is characteristic of severe depression. By contrast, in a *manic* state there may be evidence of excessive sexual drive, the apparent need for little sleep as well as a general sense of physical strength and vitality.

Although marked loss of weight is a prominent feature of *anorexia nervosa*, the patient might deny feeling hungry or ill in any way. Amenorrhea is an associated feature.

The importance of this aspect of the clinical interview is such that on its completion it is often possible to make a tentative diagnosis; it should at least be clear where the emphasis needs to be placed in the subsequent stages.

REFERENCE

ABRAHAMSON, D. (1974) Procedure Reexamined. *Lancet* **1**, 1153–4.

History-taking:
The Personal Background

The purpose of the next stage in the history is to get to know the patient as a person by building up a short biography in a systematic, mainly chronological way. The sequence should always be recorded in the same way but the amount of detail required for each stage in the biography will vary with the nature of the patient's condition and is a matter of clinical judgement.

It is best to think of the scheme as a framework in which a minimum of basic information is *always* needed but some aspects require special emphasis according to the circumstances. The main headings around which this sort of history is obtained are:
1 Family history.
2 Personal history.
3 Previous history of physical, psychiatric and forensic disorders.
4 Assessment of the patient's usual personality.

FAMILY HISTORY

As a routine some details are needed about the patient's parents and siblings. It should first be established whether his parents are alive. If not, it is important to inquire about the *age* of *death* and its *cause* as these facts can contribute to the diagnostic process. Thus it is now known that in the case of female patients, loss of a mother before the age of eleven seems to contribute to the later development of depressive illnesses. Loss of a parent in other ways may

13

also be relevant. Thus the prolonged absence of a patient's father, eg on military service, could affect personality development, as can loss of one parent due to divorce, although the nature of the parental discord may be of greater relevance than the actual fact of separation. The cause of parental death might also be of considerable importance. A history of suicide could suggest a familial illness, such as manic-depressive psychosis or schizophrenia. When possible it is useful to try to establish the patient's reaction at the time of a parent's death, and to distinguish between a normal and a pathological grief reaction, as the latter can produce a prolonged and at times severe neurotic type of illness. If the death occurred in unusually distressing circumstances it could have precipitated a post-traumatic neurosis.

It is helpful to know something of the *educational background and occupational history* of each parent, thus giving a broad indication of their intellectual level and general social adjustment, with which the patient's own attainments can be contrasted. When the patient's personal history (see below) reveals a marked discrepancy this will need to be explained. When it is judged to be of relevance, a description of each parent's usual personality characteristics should be obtained having in mind the scheme suggested below for the assessment of personality. This will include the way in which the parents related to one another, as well as to the patient and other siblings. These facts would emerge in response to such questions as 'Tell me about your father'; 'What sort of person was your mother?'; 'What sort of upbringing did you have?' and so on.

Some specific features might emerge that can have a definite impact on personality development and contribute to the later development of deviant behaviour or neurotic disorders. Thus a history of parental *violence, excessive drinking, criminal* behaviour, unduly *punitive, restrictive* or *inconsistent* attitudes or undue *leniency* might be of considerable significance.

Of particular importance is the nature of any illness from which the parents might have suffered. In the case of a *psychiatric illness* inquiry should be made about the nature of the symptoms, duration, type of treatment and outcome. The patient might even know the diagnosis and should always be asked. This might reveal a familial incidence of a condition with a definite *genetic basis* such as Huntington's chorea, in which case a very detailed family history is needed. This is usually best arranged in the form of a family tree whereby the nature of the heredity pattern can easily be seen. Functional psychoses and epilepsy can be familial as may some specific forms of mental retardation, especially if the parents are closely related.

PERSONAL HISTORY

This is the next stage in the biographical account and, as in the case of the family history, although the general outline should be the same in all cases, circumstances will dictate where special emphasis needs to be placed. The following sequence is suggested:
1 Infancy and early childhood.
2 Later childhood, adolescence and education.
3 Occupational record.
4 Sexual development and marriage.
5 Present social circumstances.

1 Infancy and childhood

The *date of birth* should first be noted. As a rule the patient will not be able to give any reliable information about his early life, although he may have been told of any unusual circumstances such as a complicated or prolonged confinement, use of forceps for the delivery, birth by Caesarian section or a very low birth weight. Such factors might be associated with a history of infantile convulsions and would suggest early brain damage due to cerebal anoxia. The temporal lobe of the brain is especially vulnerable producing a characteristic form of epilepsy in later life. It has also been postulated that some violent, explosive or antisocial behaviour can be associated with damage to one or other temporal lobes at birth.

When detailed information about this stage of development is judged to be important it has to be obtained from other sources, such as the patient's parents, other close relatives, hospital or general practitioner records.

Various aspects of *early childhood* may be relevant to the understanding of some clinical conditions. In addition to those mentioned above, the usual developmental milestones can be of importance. These include the age at which the child was able first to sit up unsupported, to crawl, walk, talk and gain control over bladder and bowels. If these are obviously delayed, some consideration of the mother's condition during pregnancy would be relevant including drug taking and exposure to infectious diseases such as rubella. These, as well as a difficult confinement, could produce brain damage resulting in varying degrees of mental handicap or on occasions contributing to certain conduct disorders that arise in childhood. The informant should also be asked whether any unusual behaviour was apparent, and specific inquiries should be made about any marked aggressive or destructive behaviour, any tendency to be overactive, or difficulties the patient might have seemed to have in relation to other people, especially other children born into the family.

2 Later childhood, adolescence and education

The period covered by this part of the history starts at the age of five when full-time education usually begins, and continues through adolescence to young adult life with the completion of the patient's education and vocational training. It is easiest to build the history around the stages of his education. With regard to his *school record,* the types of schools attended should be noted as well as his achievements not only in the academic sphere but also his relationships with other pupils, teachers and involvement in sporting and similar activities. Did he make friends easily? Was he popular? Did he belong to a gang, or group? Did he attend school regularly? Was he bullied or victimised in any way? Many patients who later show signs of having a markedly schizoid type of personality or show evidence of schizophrenia will be found to have been lonely children, experiencing difficulty in relating to their peers. The reasons for changing schools should be noted. Specific inquiry should be made into any behavioural or disciplinary problems. This information will give a basic guide to the patient's *intellectual level* and *social adjustment* at this stage of his development and where relevant, the results of any examination taken will provide additional evidence. Any prolonged periods of absence from school should be noted, together with the reasons.

Although puberty and associated sexual changes predominate in adolescence (see below), this is also a time of increasing physical strength and growing independence and a period when behavioural problems might arise. These can include experimentation with *drugs,* and other *delinquent tendencies.* Where appropriate, specific inquiry should be made about such behaviour including any history of involvement with the police.

When the patient has received a period of *higher education or training* after leaving school this should next be summarised, noting qualifications obtained, as well as the consistency or otherwise of the standards achieved. Unexpected failure or poor performance of an examination could reflect some psychiatric disability such as depression or drug or alcohol intoxication. A history of failure of early academic promise is also found in some cases of schizophrenia some time before the symptoms become evident. The way in which the patient coped with stressful experiences such as examinations and interviews should be explored, as at times the evidence of a developing phobic disorder, anxiety state or obsessional personality disorder can be revealed from such inquiries.

3 Occupational record

The next chronological stage is the patient's record on completing his full-time education or training. Note should be taken of the *types of job* he has had, their duration, reasons for change as well as any periods of *unemployment.* The patient's *income* at different stages of his career may provide a guide to his progress as well as the duties and responsibilities involved. It is often helpful to make some assessment of the way in which the patient usually copes with his work, eg whether he is overconscientious, perhaps with difficulty in delegating to others, tendency to double check things, perhaps reluctant to take holidays, all features of an obsessional personality that might become apparent from the patient's *working style*. When there is a history of frequent changes of employment the circumstances should be carefully explored, especially if due to dismissal. Some attempts should also be made to assess *job satisfaction*.

Patients who have spent any time in the army should be asked whether their health was recorded as A1 on entry and discharge. It is also helpful to find out whether they achieved promotion, and whether any disciplinary action was taken against them.

Retired people constitute an increasing proportion of the population and although they may no longer be gainfully occupied, an account should always be obtained of the way in which their time is spent and the extent to which the patient feels this meets his needs.

4 Sexual adjustment and marriage

The usual chronological sequence for information under this heading is puberty, sexual adjustment in adolescence and adult life including courtship, marriage and child rearing.

At *puberty* with the beginning of sexual awareness and interest the patient will recall his reaction to achieving a true sense of *sexual identity* and any problems it gave rise to. It may be important to clarify the way the patient was instructed in sexual matters and to establish whether the understanding is in fact adequate. Many sexual difficulties are found to arise from a surprising ignorance about the 'facts of life'. Gradually his basic sexual orientation will emerge and it is important for the examiner to establish its nature. Discussion about sexual habits needs to be approached with special discretion and the examiner should always guard against being unduly inquisitive in this area, confining himself to relevant questions only. Where relevant, however, the subject of *masturbation* should be discussed, including the nature of associated fantasies and guilt feelings, as well as the patient's early *sexual experimentation* with members of the opposite or same sex and his feelings about these experiences. The date of onset of menstruation should be asked when appropriate as well as any associated difficulties. The gradual emergence of *mature sexual behaviour* patterns should be traced, noting any special difficulties encountered and the patient's ability to develop stable, satisfactory sexual relationships should be assessed. The possibility of *sexual inadequacy* needs to be explored, especially impotence in men or frigidity in women as well as any preference for *sexually deviant* practices. Consideration must be given to those aspects of sexual behaviour that could result in a high risk of acquiring a sexually transmitted disease such as the Acquired Immune Deficiency Syndrome.

In the case of married patients, their behaviour during courtship may be of particular importance in the investigation of marital difficulties. The time the couple had known each other, and their ages and occupations at marriage should be established. This might give some general guide as to their compatibility. The general quality of the *marital relationship* should always be considered, ideally in conjunction with the patient's spouse. Specific aspects that merit detailed consideration include the adequacy of the sexual relationship, methods of contraception, the way in which roles are allocated between the partners and the extent to which each partner is involved in outside interests and relationships. This can often best be illustrated by constructing an approximate *time budget* which would show the amount of time they spend together. The possibility of extramarital relationships should be considered with discretion. These and other aspects need to be pursued as part of the process of understanding marital problems.

A note should be made of each of the patient's *children* — their present ages, educational or occupational status, health and any problems that might have existed in their development and in the relationship each child has with the patient and his spouse.

5 Present social circumstances

Following the chronological sequence the last stage in the personal history concentrates on the patient's present social circumstances. This will include his *living arrangements, present occupation,* and *leisure activities and interests.* The objective is to obtain a 'here and now' picture of his everyday life and particular emphasis on any aspects that could contribute to his disability. The adequacy of his housing and financial circumstances are especially relevant as well as his job satisfaction.

PREVIOUS HISTORY OF PHYSICAL, PSYCHIATRIC OR FORENSIC DISORDERS

Physical disorders

A brief account should next be obtained about any serious *physical illnesses, operations* or *accidents* that the patient might have experienced previously. The dates, duration and nature of any treatment should be ascertained. In normal clinical practice it is important to know the names of any hospitals at which the patient might have been treated, as it is often helpful to write for more detailed reports.

At this point in the history it is useful to ask a few screening questions about the patient's *present physical health* including any recent weight change, sleep disturbance, change in appetite or bowel habits, energy, menstrual and premenstrual problems when appropriate. Any *medication* the patient is currently taking should be carefully noted. This might include drugs that are potentially addictive such as barbiturates or amphetamines. Others can contribute to the development of depression such as certain hypotensive agents and oral contraceptives as well as barbiturates and diazepam. A schizophrenic-like psychosis can be produced by large doses of amphetamines, and confusional states by a wide range of substances including antiParkinsonian drugs and hypnotics. In addition his *smoking and drinking habits* should be noted and specific inquiries made with regard to any changes in the habitual pattern. This includes the possibility of an excessive consumption of caffeine-containing drinks such as tea, coffee or coca cola. At times, patients are rather vague or deliberately evasive about the amount of alcohol they consume. When this is judged to be relevant, the daily pattern should be noted in detail, and perhaps substantiated by considering the patient's weekly budget and the proportion spent on alcoholic drinks. If there is any suspicion of abuse of alcohol, the patient should be asked whether he drinks in the morning, if he has ever had to drink in order to control a tremor, and whether he has ever had periods of memory loss while drinking. Enquiry also needs to be made about the social consequences of excessive drinking: running into debt, losing jobs, and getting into trouble with the police. The weekly consumption of alcohol can easily be estimated by converting standard measures of alcohol beverages into units (Royal College of Psychiatrists 1986). It is helpful to apply the CAGE questionnaire (Mayfield *et al*, 1974) which identifies at-risk drinkers from general populations at a cut-off point of two or more affirmative replies to the following questions.

1   Have you ever felt you ought to cut down on your drinking?
2   Have people annoyed you by criticising your drinking?
3   Have you ever felt bad or guilty about your drinking?
4   Have you ever had a drink first thing in the morning to steady your nerves or get rid of a hangover?

Psychiatric disorders

This aspect of the history is of particular importance and contributes greatly to the diagnostic process. As in the case of previous physical illnesses the patient should be asked about previous mental disorders. When possible the *dates and duration* should be noted, as well as the names of *hospitals* at which he was treated and the *nature of the treatment*. Spells of treatment from the

21

patient's family doctor should also be considered as it is well established that most psychiatric disorders are treated in that setting. Often the patients will know the diagnosis but if not, their recall of the symptoms is usually helpful. These episodes should be noted in chronological order as well as any unusual circumstances in which the illness seemed to develop. Hospital records should always be requested where circumstances permit.

In addition to well defined earlier episodes, the patient should be asked whether he has experienced any psychiatric *symptoms* previously as these might not have been formally recognised at the time. Examples are often helpful: 'Have you ever had any unusual experiences or feelings you didn't understand?'; 'Have you ever been depressed or excited for no apparent reason?'; 'Have you ever had any special fears or phobias?' The dates of such experiences should be noted as well as their duration and associated circumstances. Details of past *suicidal behaviour* should also be recorded.

Forensic disorders

Under this heading would be included details of an occasion on which the patient might have committed an *offence* or *behaved in some illegal* or *antisocial* way whether or not such behaviour was detected. This information overlaps with the assessment of personality (see below) and previous psychiatric history, as on occasions such behaviour is symptomatic of mental disorder.

The approximate dates of *prosecutions*, outcome including nature of any *sentence* and when this is custodial, the patient's reaction to such experiences should be recorded. Other details will include any history of taking cannabis or drugs of dependency, LSD and similar psychotomimetic substances. Misuse of other drugs such as analgesics, hypnotics and narcotics should be included.

ASSESSMENT OF THE PATIENT'S USUAL PERSONALITY

This is perhaps the most difficult and least reliable aspect of the history and can rarely be adequately completed without an informant's assistance in providing a more objective account. Nevertheless, it is important to make some assessment of the patient's usual personality characteristics and although there is no generally agreed method of achieving this, the following scheme is suggested as being relevant to most clinical situations.

Firstly, the examiner should become familiar with the account given of the main personality disorders in the Tenth Revision of the International Classification of Diseases (1989 Draft of Chapter V World Health Organization Geneva 1989). These are *paranoid, schizoid, dyssocial, emotionally unstable, histrionic, anankostic (obsessive-compulsive), anxious (avoidant), dependent,* and *cyclothymic* personality disorders.

Once familiar with each of these categories it becomes possible to ask a few simple screening questions relevant to each category, in order to find out if the patient's personality conforms in any way to one or more of these personality types. If so, it is then necessary to decide whether the prominence of the traits identified is such as to justify a diagnosis of 'personality disorder' as defined in the diagnostic guidelines of the ICD-10. When this is applicable the particular personality type to which the patient's personality characteristics approximate should be noted.

In considering these various types of personality disorder the following examples of screening questions could be used:

Paranoid personality disorder
How do you get on with other people?
Do you find you can trust people?
Do you sometimes feel picked upon?
Do you think people like you generally?
Are you self-conscious?
Are you mostly treated fairly?

Schizoid personality disorder
Do you have many friends?
Can you mix easily?
Do you prefer to be alone or with company?
Would you describe yourself as shy?

Dyssocial personality disorder
Have you been in much trouble with the police?
How do you get on with people in authority?
Do you dislike being told what to do?
Do you have impulses to hurt people?

Emotionally unstable personality disorder
Do you ever get into an uncontrollable rage?
Have you ever hurt anyone or caused any serious damage?
Do you frequently lose your temper?

Histrionic personality disorder
Are you sometimes overemotional?
Do you like to be the centre of attention?
Do you find it easy to act a part?
Do you tend to rely on other people a great deal?

Anankastic (obsessive-compulsive) personality disorder
Do you always try to follow a set routine?
Do you prefer things to be very neat and tidy?
Are you always punctual?
Do you ever tend to check things more than once or twice?
Are you exceptionally houseproud?

Anxious (avoidant) personality disorder
Do you tend to feel very tense and self-conscious?
Do you live cautiously and avoid taking unnecessary risks?
Are you concerned that you might not be popular?

Dependent personality disorder
Do you tend to rely on others excessively?
Do you prefer others to make decisions for you?
Do you often feel helpless on your own?

Cyclothymic personality disorder
Is your mood stable, or does it fluctuate greatly from day-to-day?
Would you describe yourself as a happy and contented person?
Do you usually hope for the best or expect the worst?
Do people think of you as a happy-go-lucky person, the life-and-soul of the party or perhaps rather gloomy and unhappy?

Considerable flexibility will be needed in the way the questions are asked and the answers must be supplemented by information derived from the history.

REFERENCES

MAYFIELD, D., McCLEOD, G. & HALL, P. (1974) The CAGE questionnaire: Validation of a new alcoholism screening questionnaire. *American Journal of Psychiatry*, **131**, 1121–3.
ROYAL COLLEGE OF PSYCHIATRISTS (1986) *Alcohol Our Favourite Drug*. Tavistock, London.
WORLD HEALTH ORGANISATION (1989) *Mental Disorders: Glossary and Guide to their Classification in accordance with the Tenth Revision of the International Classification of Diseases*. World Health Organisation, Geneva.

Present Mental State

Many signs and symptoms will already have been noted by the interviewer both during the initial observation of the patient and while taking the history (see Chapters Two and Three). By the time he has completed the history he should have a range of possible diagnoses in mind, or may indeed have already settled on the most likely diagnosis. Assessment of the present mental state is therefore often a confirmatory rather than an exploratory procedure.

Assessment begins from the first moment the patient is seen. This may be when the psychiatrist meets the patient in the waiting area and escorts him to the consulting room, or when the patient enters the consulting room, depending on the psychiatrist's practice. Very important observations are often made at this stage, before there is any verbal interchange between patient and psychiatrist and can help considerably towards making a diagnosis. These observations are usually made by the psychiatrist unconsciously, but if the non-verbal attributes of the patient are assessed in a conscious and systematic way then they can be used more effectively and there will also be less chance of missing significant features. They represent additional clues to be used in conjunction with the rest of the interview in the process of reaching a diagnosis.

NON-VERBAL BEHAVIOUR

DRESS

Nowadays dress is much less formal and conventional than it used

27

to be. Nevertheless, a markedly unusual appearance can still provide useful clues to diagnosis.

Self-neglect

Men may appear unshaven and in both sexes it may be evident that the face has not been washed, or the hair combed. Women may wear no makeup (although this may be currently fashionable) or else may have applied makeup carelessly. It should be noted that obvious neglect of grooming is not common in hospitalised patients as nurses usually supervise these activities. Observe whether the finger nails are long and dirty, or bitten to the quick. Dress may be untidy with buttons undone or done up incorrectly. Clothing may be stained, worn or torn. It may also be inadequate for the weather. Self-neglect can occur in *depression, schizophrenia* and *dementia*.

Colour

This is commonly drab in *depressed* patients and bright in *manics*. Manics may also wear clashing colours.

Unusual combinations of clothing

The wearing of a jacket and no shirt or a coat on backwards is sometimes seen in *schizophrenia*, where it has a symbolic significance, or in *dementia*, where it is indicative of apraxia. Schizophrenic patients may also don additional items of clothing for symbolic reasons, for example a scarf tied round the forehead to indicate royalty.

Dress inappropriate for age

Some adults wear childish clothes, for example a middleaged woman wearing teenage clothing, or style their hair in a childish way, for example a topknot with a large bow. This may be indicative of *emotional immaturity*.

Dress inappropriate for sex

Transsexual and *transvestite* men wear women's clothes and makeup and sometimes speak in a high voice. The transformation may be skilful enough to deceive even an experienced psychiatrist.

Unusual accessories

Schizophrenic patients sometimes pack their pockets with their belongings or carry a large holdall full of personal possessions or papers and manuscripts. They may also carry objects of symbolic significance, such as a stick with a ball tied to it to simulate a sceptre.

GAIT

One advantage of collecting the patient from the waiting area is that it gives the psychiatrist an opportunity to observe any abnormalities of gait. This can also be achieved in the consulting room but the distance from door to chair may be too short to allow useful observations.

Unusually slow

This may be indicative of depression or Parkinsonism. *Depressed* patients may walk slowly with head bent forward, eyes downcast and shoulders hunched. The motor retardation is often associated with slow speech and delay in answering questions. *Parkinsonism* gives rise to a slow, rigid gait in which the limbs are moved stiffly and the head faces directly forward with unblinking eyes. There is a reduction in associated movements, so that the arms may not swing during walking. Parkinsonism may result from phenothiazine medication or may be seen in association with dementing conditions. Some patients with Parkinson's disease may present to the psychiatrist with depression.

Unusually fast

Some *manic* patients walk briskly. Very excited patients may dance or skip. Excessive motor activity in manic patients is often associated with rapid and excessive speech.

Unusual character

Characteristic gaits may be seen in phobia, hysteria, schizophrenia and obsessional neurosis. The *agoraphobic* patient may walk close to the wall, maintaining contact with it with one hand. Sometimes she insists on being accompanied by the person she relies on habitually to go out with. *Hysterics* may show a broad-based staggering gait, sometimes collapsing at intervals and clinging to the nearest person for support. *Schizophrenia* gives rise to a variety of abnormalities of gait. Mannerisms may affect the gait, for example, taking one step backwards after every fifth pace. *Catatonia* can produce a sudden freezing in the middle of walking. Ambitendence is shown by alternating entering the leaving movements at the entrance of the room. *Obsessional* patients may avoid treading on cracks in a tiled floor or touching door knobs, and sometimes go out of their way to avoid physical contact with other people near them.

MOTOR ACTIVITY

It should be noted whether the patient is underactive or overactive. Normal people move about a moderate amount during an interview. They shift their position from time-to-time to get more comfortable, cross and uncross their legs, lean forward when discussing important issues, and use their hands to emphasise what they are saying, or to light cigarettes if they smoke. The patient who shows none of this, but who sits perfectly still throughout the interview, is abnormally underactive. This may result from the retardation of severe *depression,* from *Parkinsonism,* either *drug induced* or associated with *organic brain disease,* or may indicate *catatonic stupor.*

Overactivity may be manifested by an increase in the quantity of movements or by a change in their quality. There may simply be an exaggeration of the normal movements described above. The hands may be in continual motion, fidgeting with each other or with a convenient object; the patient may constantly shift his position or keep leaning backwards and forwards. This is seen in *anxiety states*, where a coarse tremor of the hands may also be observed, and in *agitated depression*, where the patient characteristically wrings his hands continually. Restlessness of the legs alone is usually due to trifluoperazine or related compounds and is known as *akathisia*.

Extreme forms of overactivity are seen in patients who leave their seats and move about the interview room. Repetitive pacing up and down is usually a manifestation of *agitated depression* and is accompanied by a depressed facies. Aimless movement is shown by patients with *akathisia*, who usually explain their need to walk about by saying that they can't keep their legs still. Skipping, dancing, acrobatics, and other exuberant forms of activity are seen in *mania*. Sudden bursts of physical overactivity which may involve destructiveness and aggression are seen in *catatonia* and either precede or follow stupor. However, this is now very rare in western countries.

Some patients respond to auditory hallucinations with non-verbal behaviour only. They may move their lips as though speaking but without uttering a sound. They may also turn their head suddenly as though to a source of sound unheard by the interviewer, or may restrict this response to a sudden flicking of the eyes sideways or upwards. This may be followed by soundless muttering. Some patients get up suddenly, as though in response to a command, and may stand motionless in a listening attitude. Motor behaviour of an abnormal form may be categorised as:

1   Tics — irregular repetitive movements that may involve a small group of muscles, for example, twitching of one eyelid, or several large groups, for example, twitching of the head to one side and elevation of the shoulder. They may be unilateral or bilateral and often become more exaggerated and more frequent when attention is drawn to them.

2 Tardive dyskinesia — one of the more serious side-effects of phenothiazine medication. It usually affects the mouth and tongue, which are occupied in ceaseless sinuous movements. These may be severe enough to interfere with speech, eating and swallowing. Sometimes the chest muscles are also involved, producing irregular, jerky respirations.

3 Stereotypies — regular repetitive movements without any obvious symbolic meaning for the patient, for example, rocking backwards and forwards, continuously rotating the head to one side, tapping one foot on the floor.

4 Mannerisms — stylised movements that may have a recognisable significance in another context, for example, saluting or blessing with the hand, or may have an idiosyncratic meaning for the patient, for example, stamping the foot three times.

5 Posturing — the patient maintains an unusual and awkward posture for a considerable period of time, for example, standing on one foot with the other leg raised in the air.

6 Negativism — the patient does exactly the opposite of what is asked, or else fails to respond to any request by the interviewer, for example, to sit down.

7 Ambitendence — the patient alternates between opposing movements, for example, advancing and withdrawing motions on the threshold of the interview room.

8 Waxy flexibility — the patient's limbs and head remain in whatever position the interviewer places them and muscle tone is uniformly increased. These imposed postures can be maintained for long periods.

9 Echopraxia — the patient exactly imitates the interviewer's movements.

10 Resistiveness — the patient actively resists attempts by the interviewer to move him.

Tics can occur as an isolated symptom, may be combined with coprolalia in *Gilles de la Tourette's syndrome,* or may be part of an *anxiety state.* Tardive dyskinesia is iatrogenic.

Stereotypies occur in *infantile autism,* in association with *mental retardation,* and in *schizophrenia.* The remaining abnormalities of motor behaviour are characteristic of *schizophrenia,* but occur rarely.

SOCIAL MANNER

The patient's social behaviour can be observed in two situations; in the waiting area, where his relationship to other patients and relatives can be assessed, and on meeting the doctor.

Diminished social contact

Patients suffering from *depression* or *schizophrenia* tend to be socially withdrawn and are unlikely to make contact with other people in the waiting area. Most patients manage a social smile on meeting the doctor, but this may be beyond the severely depressed patient and the schizophrenic with flat affect. The patient with paranoid symptoms may have a guarded, hesitant attitude.

Increased social contact

Manic patients engage everyone around in conversation and may speak in a loud voice. They may be overeffusive or overfamiliar with the doctor and attempt to take over his role. They sometimes make inappropriate sexual advances to staff or to other patients.

Inappropriate social behaviour

Some patients appear puzzled by everything that is going on around them. They don't seem to understand what is expected of them and either make inappropriate social responses or more usually fail to make the expected responses. This can occur when the patient's intellectual level is inadequate, as in *mental retardation* and *dementia,* or when cerebral function is disturbed, as in *organic confusional states.* It may also accompany the perplexity that occurs in some *acute functional psychoses.*

NON-VERBAL EXPRESSION OF AFFECT

The patient's affective state manifests itself in non-verbal as well as verbal behaviour. Facial expression is the most obvious non-verbal index of the patient's mood, but body posture and limb movements also reflect this. The interviewer will have had plenty of opportunity to observe these features during the history-taking.

When *depressive affect* is present the eyebrows are drawn together and their inner ends are raised obliquely. This movement deepens the vertical furrow between them and forms transverse furrows across the middle part only of the forehead. This produces the T-sign of depression. The eyelids are drawn together, narrowing the palpebral fissure, while the corners of the mouth are drawn down. The patient may cry openly but in the absence of weeping the eyes may glisten with unshed tears. Eye contact with the examiner is avoided and the gaze is usually directed at the ground. The head is bent forward and drawn down to the shoulders, which are hunched up. The arms are kept close to the body, which may also lean forward (Figure 4.1).

Severely depressed patients may exhibit a fixed expression of misery on their faces. The immobility of their expression sometimes causes confusion with the blank face of the *emotionally blunted* patient. However, although the expression in both cases is unchanging, the face of the depressive bears many marks of expression which convey persistent sadness, whereas the face of the affectively flattened patient is devoid of expression marks and suggests no emotion whatsoever. During normal conversation, the participants smile at each other from time to time in order to reinforce social contact. Failure to smile at all during the interview occurs both with depression and blunted affect.

In *anxious* patients the eyebrows are raised, deepening the horizontal furrows in the forehead and widening the palpebral fissure. The pupils are dilated and the mouth is slightly opened. The body is often held rigidly upright and a coarse tremor of the hands is apparent (Figure 4.2). Respiratory movements are fast

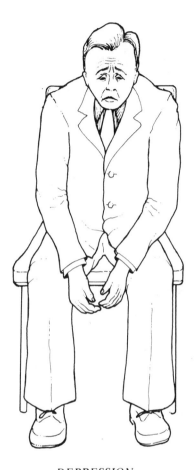

DEPRESSION

Figure 4.1

Face: Eyebrows drawn together, medial ends raised obliquely. Forehead shows vertical furrows and horizontal furrows across middle part. Corners of eyes and mouth turn down.
Posture: Head bent forward, gaze directed at ground, shoulders hunched, arms close to body, body bent forward.

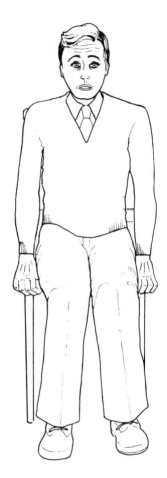

ANXIETY

Figure 4.2

Face: Eyebrows raised, horizontal furrows right across forehead. Eyes wide open, pupils dilated. Lips slightly parted.
Posture: Body held rigidly upright, hands gripping chair, knees pressed together.

and shallow, and perspiration may be observed on the patient's face.

Rage or *anger* in a patient are instantly recognisable, but minor degrees of *irritability* may be overlooked. They are indicated by slight retraction of the lips, exposing the teeth which are clenched, eyebrows lowered over wide open eyes, and distension of the nostrils. The shoulders and arms are often held rigid and the fists clenched.

PERPLEXITY

Figure 4.3

Face: Eyebrows lowered. Forehead shows vertical furrows. Lower eyelids raised and wrinkled, roaming gaze. Hand raised to mouth.

Hypomanic mood is indicated by a cheerful, smiling expression for much of the interview. This is in harmony with the content of the patient's speech, which often includes jokes and puns, and expressions of well-being. These patients make direct eye contact with the interviewer and usually succeed in communicating their elevated mood to him. This is in contrast to the patient with *incongruity of affect,* who laughs, giggles or smiles to himself, often without making eye contact with the interviewer. These patients seem to be amused by some private joke and do not communicate any sense of elevated mood to the interviewer. At times they may cry or wail when the content of their speech is neutral or even pleasant.

In a patient showing *perplexity,* the eyebrows are lowered and brought together in a frown, producing vertical furrows on the forehead. The lower eyelids are generally raised and wrinkled and the patient's gaze roams about the room vacantly without focusing on anything. The patient may rub his eyes or his forehead with his hand or may raise his hand to his mouth or chin (Figure 4.3). This affective state is often accompanied by delusional mood and commonly precedes the development of a frank psychosis.

Suspicious patients may narrow their eyes and dart sideways glances at the interviewer or at features of the room, but suspicion is easier to detect from the patient's questions and attitude to the interview than from his non-verbal behaviour.

The affective states dealt with above, have each been described in their pure form, but it must be recognised that patients usually show a mixture of several affects which makes assessment more difficult. If the patient's affect fluctuates from one extreme to another throughout the interview he is showing *lability of mood* which indicates a mixed affective state or an organic cerebral condition. The former is characteristically seen in patients who are predominantly manic but are moved to tears suddenly and briefly from time to time.

FACTORS PREVENTING AN INTERVIEW FROM BEING COMPLETED

Before going on to discuss verbal behaviour it is necessary to consider features of the patient's behaviour which may prevent a full interview being conducted.

Overactivity: patients with catatonic excitement, mania, or agitated depression may be unable to sit still long enough for the interviewer to ask the necessary questions. The examination should be completed when the overactivity is controlled by treatment.

Muteness: the patient who is completely or nearly mute cannot be questioned in the usual way. The interviewer will have to wait until speech returns spontaneously or following treatment.

Poor concentration: a number of psychiatric conditions may so impair concentration that the patient is unable to attend to questions long enough to answer them. The retardation of cognitive processes accompanying severe depression can have this effect; so may an intense preoccupation with delusions or hallucinations. Organic cerebral conditions may lower the level of consciousness with a resulting impairment in concentration.

Distractability: patients suffering from mania are very easily distracted from attending to the interviewer by events outside the interview. They readily turn their attention to the interviewer's dress, other people present, objects in the room, or noises outside the room.

Attitude to the interview: suspicious or hostile patients may refuse to answer questions. Manic patients may attempt to reverse roles, and start interrogating the interviewer. Compliant patients may answer yes to everything, while malingerers may be deliberately misleading. Severely obsessional patients may be completely unable to decide whether the answer to a particular question is yes or no, or may take a great deal of time coming to a conclusion.

Speech disorder: the speech of manic and schizophrenic patients may be so disordered that the interviewer is unable to get satisfactory answers to his questions.

Foreign born: a language barrier may make questioning impossible. A fluent interpreter should be obtained.

The deaf: partially deaf patients usually have hearing aids, which should be used during the interview. Completely deaf patients may understand sign language in which case an interpreter should be brought in.

The interviewing of difficult patients is dealt with in Chapter Nine.

VERBAL BEHAVIOUR

Speech being a form of motor activity exhibits the same kinds of abnormality that affect movement, so that changes may occur in the rate or quantity of speech. In addition, volume and tone may be altered in certain psychiatric states.

Rate and quantity of speech

Speech may be too slow or too fast, too little or too much. Slow speech is a manifestation of the psychomotor retardation that accompanies *depression,* usually of the most severe kind. Not only are the words spoken more slowly, but the pauses between the words are lengthened and so is the pause before answering. Indeed sometimes these patients do not answer at all and the question has to be repeated. The quantity of speech is reduced in *depression* so that the patient often restricts his answer to the minimum number of words necessary, without any elaboration. In extreme forms this may mean only monosyllabic replies — yes, no or maybe, or no response at all, in which case the patient is described as mute.

Fast speech is characteristic of *manic* patients. Not only do they speak too fast, but also excessively. It is often difficult for the interviewer to get a word in edgeways, as these patients may not pause to allow the customary dialogue to take place.

Obsessional patients may also speak more than the situation demands. They tend to get bogged down in the details of their answer and to be unable to bring their remarks to a conclusion as they are continually modifying what they have just said. Unlike manic patients, however, their speech is neither too fast nor too loud. Furthermore they talk round and round the same point, whereas manic patients are constantly changing from topic-to-topic.

Volume and tone of speech

The volume is often reduced in *depression,* whereas *manic* patients may speak louder than necessary. Depression is also characterised by a change in respiration which affects speech. This is exemplified by sighing, a form of non-verbal behaviour which sometimes punctuates the speech of depressed patients. A sigh is a prolonged expiration in which virtually the whole content of the lungs is expelled. In normal respiration, full expiration is inhibited so that enough pressure remains in the lungs to maintain the voice at a steady volume and pitch. The failure to do this in depression results in a characteristic drop in volume and pitch at the end of an utterance. The listener gains the impression of a mournful cadence.

The normal variation in the tone of voice tends to be restricted in depressed patients, whose speech is also typically low-pitched. A monotonous voice is also found in patients with *blunted affect,* and although they show no lowering of pitch, the two kinds of voice are not easy to distinguish.

Non-social speech

This is present when the patient talks to himself. This may be in the form of whispering, muttering, talking out aloud, or even shouting. It is indicative of the presence of auditory hallucinations.

Neologisms

Speech develops to communicate experiences that people share in common. The experiences of psychotic patients are outside the range of most people and hence words are not readily available for their expression. Therefore it is not surprising that they often have to push language to its limit and beyond to convey their psychotic experiences to the non-psychotic. This results in the idiosyncratic use of ordinary words and the invention of new words or neologisms. An example of the former is provided by the patient who complained that 'my sister trades on my brain'. By this phrase she meant to convey the experience that her mental activities were intruded on.

Neologisms may be derived from recognisable words, as with 'acousticals' for auditory hallucinations, or may be completely new inventions, for example 'living is that perexis'. Some patients, when asked, can explain what their neologisms mean in ordinary words; others find it impossible to do so. Neologisms are characteristic of *schizophrenia*.

Speech disorder

Psychotic patients exhibit speech disorder of various kinds. This is usually assumed to be a product of disturbed thought processes and for this reason is often referred to as thought disorder. However, this term is also used for the various abnormal experiences that patients complain of in reference to their thoughts, such as thought withdrawal, thought insertion and thought broadcast. These will be discussed in Chapter Five. To avoid confusing these different phenomena, the term *speech disorder* will be used to refer to disturbed speech instead of the term thought disorder. The same disturbances that affect speech may of course be evident in writing.

Speech disorder is an uncommon symptom which may occur in *mania* and *schizophrenia*. The interviewer should be alerted to the possibility of speech disorder if he has difficulty in understanding what the patient is saying. This may be due to abrupt shifts in topic or to a vagueness and lack of focus.

Shifts in topic

These may occur without any logical connection between one topic and the next. This is characteristic of *schizophrenia* and is termed *knight's move* or *derailment of the train of thought*. It may occur between two sentences or in the middle of a sentence. The following example illustrates shifts in topic between two adjacent sentences and within a sentence.

'I have this anxiety because I have done a lot of medical work, but also against drugs. And just, well I mean the world goes round and I think the most important thing is to bring up children and look after them in their childhood.'

The next example demonstrates a number of abrupt shifts within sentences.

'I'm sorry it happens but this is in, saved by seconds, you see. They think this is ridiculous, the Americans, Canadians and the English and the Europeans and so forth and so on. And damn good ideas at that time as well, and I'm just getting my voice back.'

In this extract the grammatical structure of speech remains relatively intact, but if the process of fragmentation goes much further, then the grammar begins to disintegrate and speech becomes a mere stringing together of unrelated words. This is known as a *word salad* or *verbigeration*.

The following example illustrates a distorted grammatical structure although the process has not developed quite as far as verbigeration.

'And to get them prepared unto on and then when the lord is ready, that gist that's back in my head, when the lord says so, my lord there's then supplied the people who, who's ready to, who have been applied to come in and coincide their in on the thing the lord bringeth forth to, for me to say on that day, on how and how and there and when to coincide their in unto with me.'

Minor degrees of knight's move may not become apparent unless the patient is allowed to go on talking without interruption for some minutes. It appears that the further the patient drifts from the anchor of the interviewer's question, the more fragmented his thinking, and hence, his speech becomes.

Sometimes the shift in topic occurs between the interviewer's question and the patient's answer, so that the latter seems to be quite unrelated to the former. The following is an example of answering off the point:

'What kinds of things are you interested in nowadays?'

'The ring o' roses, hip, hip, hooray he's down dead, we die.'

Patients with *mania* also exhibit shifts in topic while speaking, but there is some understandable connection linking one topic with the next. This may be in the form of words rhyming (clang associations), words sounding similar (assonance), words with more than one meaning (punning), or word association. The shifting from topic-to-topic by means of such connections is known as *flight of ideas*. The following extract demonstrates a shift in topic occasioned by word association.

'I've been very, very angry and broody. Yes, broody is the right word, like a chicken. Yes, broody chicken. We had chickens in our backyard during the war. It is one of the reasons why mum and I stayed alive.'

The next example illustrates word associations and punning.

'The only thing I really worry about is utterly locked up doors which you can't get out of at all. It's the locking up, the screwing up. The only thing I can't stand is a totally screwy situation and my family, my mother and my father, are the most totally screwy people.'

The following extract contains word association, (blue-green, protective-warning), rhyming (nice-device), and assonance (warning-warm).

'That looks blue, that doesn't upset me at all. It's green, it's nice, it's a protective device. Warmth and comfort with the warning of blue on the end and a nice warm ....'

Disturbed speech in *schizophrenia* sometimes also demonstrates clang associations, assonance, punning and word association. However, these devices appear as isolated fragments rather than lubricating the flow of ideas as they do in *mania*. This is illustrated by the following examples of schizophrenic speech.

'I think I'm quite sane. I don't believe in insanity. Sanatoriums, yes, It's people looking for fresh air. Unless we whiff up our nostrils. It makes you feel good.'

'Now this reminds me of Robert Burns, or Rabbie Burns, Rabbie, rabbi, rabbits, mooses, mice.'

'It's got nothing to do with, behind, drop dead one day with surprise, because he'd bought the same oilheater as I had, and put it gently by, as I did to his. Winks, blinks. It's called Dutch, sir, because I'm going Holland today. Home on lovely evening. Evening lovely. Captain steps, final chippings. Saved by the clock, sir. Switch is. We won't talk. We'll simply say, sit back, behaviour normal, snail's pace.'

It should be noted that the distinction made between knight's move and flight of ideas depends on the interviewer being able to appreciate the connections between consecutive topics in the latter form of speech but not in the former. This may be very difficult when listening to extreme forms of manic speech, where not only are shifts of topic occurring all the time, but the pace of speech is very rapid. In such cases, if the speech is of crucial diagnostic significance, it is worth tape-recording a sample and transcribing it at leisure.

Vagueness

Another type of speech disorder, seen in *schizophrenia,* is distinguished by a lack of focus on any particular topic, so that although the patient speaks grammatically and logically, little or no information is imparted to the listener. This is known as *poverty of content* and is exemplified by the following.

'What are your plans for the future?'

'Well, a bit varied, but I've got an idea that I could sort of try and take on, after thinking really now, that if I went home after, perhaps after this party on, after a good few days, I think I'm late about this party, that's the other fear, but perhaps after that, if I may see the doctor. I've been going up there for a bit. But I plan to go home first and think about things for a little while.'

45

If the patient's speech is too disordered for the interviewer to get coherent answers to his questions, then he has to resort to alternative strategies. These are dealt with in Chapter Nine. If speech is reasonably normal, then the interviewer can proceed to elicit further symptoms by questioning the patient.

The Eliciting of Symptoms: Delusions

It has been shown that a psychiatrist usually makes up his mind about the diagnosis within five minutes of first seeing the patient. This indicates the amount of information that is often obtained from the patient's appearance and non-verbal behaviour and from his presenting complaints. However, it also reflects the pressure of time under which most clinicians work. The diagnostic process in psychiatry is generally a hierarchical one, with the search for significant symptoms occurring in a stepwise manner. In younger patients top priority tends to be given to evidence of schizophrenia, which is sought for first. If this is absent, then the psychiatrist looks for indications of the other functional psychoses. If there is no suggestion of a psychotic illness, then neurotic symptoms are focused on. If the psychiatrist decides there is good evidence for schizophrenia then he usually looks no further, and is very unlikely to proceed down the diagnostic ladder to ask about neurotic symptoms. While this may be justified by restrictions on time, it can lead to important omissions. For example, when one inquires about the whole range of symptoms in schizophrenic patients, as in assessment for a research study, one encounters significant depressive symptoms in over half. This is not only of theoretical importance, but may indicate which patients are most at risk of suicide, a frequent cause of death in schizophrenia.

For these reasons it is essential to ask screening questions in all areas of symptomatology. These need not be very detailed but should be sufficiently comprehensive so that negative answers will

47

exclude any major symptoms in each area. The kind of screening questions required will be discussed in relation to each area of symptomatology.

The information obtained by the psychiatrist during the history-taking should already have indicated the most important areas of symptomatology for the particular patient. It is sensible to inquire about these areas first before asking screening questions in any other areas. Apart from other considerations, this is what the patient expects, so that this way of proceeding is most likely to gain his cooperation. However, some psychiatrists prefer to have a set order of asking questions which they follow each time, regardless of the patient's main symptoms. This is a matter of personal interviewing style, and the individual psychiatrist should adopt the method he feels most comfortable with.

In a book the various areas of symptomatology have to be set out in some order, and here they will be dealt with in a hierarchical way following the sequence of the customary diagnostic process. Hence the first area to be considered will be that of delusions.

In the case of each symptom an attempt is made to convey the essence of the symptom by a phenomenological description and by examples drawn from interviews with patients. It is left up to the reader to construct his own questions on this basis.

In formulating questions, it is important to be aware of a number of problems. Firstly, there is the issue of social conformity. The patient will usually be at a social disadvantage by comparison with the doctor. This is partly because he is likely to come from a lower social class than the doctor and partly because of his role as a patient. One consequence of this is that he will tend to give the answers that he thinks the doctor expects. Therefore, the doctor must be careful to avoid implying any expectations in his questions. The question — 'You don't hear voices, do you?' — implies the answer, no; whereas the question — 'You do hear voices, don't you?' — implies the answer, yes. The interviewer should phrase his questions neutrally — 'Do you hear voices?' — without any implied answer.

Secondly, the interviewer should avoid jargon and should use the patient's vocabulary as far as possible. Never ask — 'Do you have hallucinations?' — but rather — 'Do you hear voices?' Thirdly, the interviewer should not accept a simple 'yes' as evidence for the presence of symptoms, particularly those of major diagnostic significance. He should go on to question the patient closely until he is convinced that the patient's account of his experience meets the phenomenological criteria for the symptom. Two clinical examples of this crossquestioning approach follow.

Example 1

Interviewer: Do you ever find that your thoughts stop dead and leave your mind a complete blank?
Patient: This happens sometimes, yes.
I: What is it like?
P: It's not very good. You're just drifting around like a leaf.
I: Is it just that your thoughts drift off what you were thinking about or do they actually disappear?
P: Your mind just goes more or less blank. You just sort of tick over.
I: Is it as though your thoughts have been taken away or is it just that they've stopped?
P: No, not taken away. It's just as though they've stopped for a little while.
Comment: This patient describes thought block but not thought withdrawal (see p. 54).

Example 2

Interviewer: Do you ever feel controlled from outside like a puppet or robot?
Patient: Yes, oh yes, definitely. I get the impression that there are people who are greater than I am who are therefore controlling me. It is true. People are controlled. I don't think there's much argument about this really.
I: Of course some people are controlled by money or by force of

character, but do you ever get the feeling that your arms and legs are being moved for you or your voice used?
P: Nothing like that. Only an indirect control.
I: Do you ever feel completely possessed by another person?
P: Not possessed, no. Influenced more. People with more power than you can influence you.
I: How do they exert this influence?
P: By giving you their views.
Comment: This patient has *not* got delusions of control (see p. 55).

DELUSIONS

A delusion is a false belief, firmly held by the patient, which is not consistent with the information available to him and with the beliefs of his cultural group, and which cannot be dispelled by argument or proof to the contrary. Patients who concede under questioning that their delusions might be mistaken, due to their imagination, or part of a psychiatric illness are suffering from *partial delusions.* Patients whose false beliefs cannot be shaken by argument have *full delusions.* It is essential to view the patient's beliefs in relation to the information available to him and to the beliefs that are current in his cultural group. For example, if you stopped someone in the streets of London in the sixteenth century and asked him if a man could fly through the air he would tell you that it was impossible except with the aid of witchcraft. A belief in witches was widespread in sixteenth century England, so this citizen could not be called deluded by the standards of his time and place. The Londoner of today, asked the same question, will reply that of course man can fly, and if pressed will almost certainly deny the existence of witchcraft. However, three classes of people today might express a belief in witchcraft. One class consists of native born English people who still believe in witchcraft. Such groups exist in modern England and even practise the rites of witches in associations called covens. A second class consists of immigrants to England from parts of the world where a belief in witches still flourishes. Africa and the West Indies are examples of such places. The third group is made up of people who are deluded.

It is clear then that in order to decide whether a patient is expressing delusional beliefs, it is necessary to have some information about the beliefs of people belonging to the same cultural group. For example, it may be important to know whether members of the patient's family believe in spiritualism and thought reading, or whether the patient belongs to a religious sect which encourages 'speaking in tongues' as a manifestation of religious fervour. The question arises of how large has the group of people to be who share the patient's belief before it can be discounted as delusional. Certainly one other person is not enough. In the situation in which two people share a very unusual belief, for example that there are microphones hidden in the walls of their house, it is likely that one of them is mentally ill and has imposed his or her delusion on the other. In these cases of *folie à deux*, as they are known, the non-patient is usually of low intelligence or is dependent on the patient for some other reason. Cases of *folie à trois* (three people involved) and *folie à quatre* (four people involved) have been recorded, but once half a dozen or more people share an unusual belief it is likely to be subcultural and within the range of normal behaviour rather than a delusion originated by one member and adopted by the others.

Of course it is always possible for a person to be a member of a small sect with unusual beliefs *and* to be deluded. In fact it is likely that some people with delusions seek social groups in which their delusional beliefs will be more or less acceptable. However, there is usually some way in which the patient's delusions diverge from the beliefs held by other members of the sect. It is therefore worth gaining the cooperation of another member of the sect in these cases and asking them what they think of the beliefs of the patient that the doctor suspects may be delusional.

Chapter Five

TYPES OF DELUSIONS

Delusions of thought interference

The five types of delusions dealt with under this heading are of great importance in the diagnosis of schizophrenia as they include a number of Schneider's first rank symptoms, which are widely used to make this diagnosis. If the patient has not already given evidence of these types of delusions, he should be asked a screening question as to whether he has experienced any interference with his thoughts. If he answers 'no', but the interviewer strongly suspects schizophrenia, he should go on to ask about the more detailed symptoms that follow.

1 Delusion of thought insertion

The patient experiences thoughts in his mind which he does not recognise as originating in his own thought processes. If he is nevertheless prepared to accept that they might be his own thoughts, or the products of his unconscious mind, then he has not got the fully developed delusion but a partial form of it. For the full delusion to be present, the patient must state definitely that there are thoughts in his mind which do not belong to him. Many patients with this symptom say that these alien thoughts come from outside themselves and are inserted into their mind. The full delusion is a Schneiderian first rank symptom.

Clinical examples
'It appeared that people's thoughts were being transferred into my mind.'
'People try to force thoughts into my mind.'
'Thoughts come into my mind from outer space.'
'I'm picking up thoughts from other people. It's like being a receiving station.'

2 Delusion of thought broadcast

This is the reverse of the previous symptom. Instead of experiencing thoughts from outside being inserted into his mind, the patient feels that his thoughts are transmitted to other people. A belief in telepathy is quite widespread among normal people, and could be confused with this symptom. A distinction between the two can be made on the following grounds. People who believe in telepathy claim that they can project their thoughts into other people's minds, but do not describe the *experience* of thoughts actually leaving their mind, whereas this is the essence of thought broadcast. Most telepaths have to concentrate, meditate or in some way alter their normal mental state in order to achieve the thought transfer they claim, whereas thought broadcast is almost always a passive experience which occurs involuntarily. The occasional patient believes he can exert control over the transfer of his thoughts. As a corollary of this, telepaths either value the powers they claim or adopt a neutral attitude towards them, while patients with thought broadcast often complain about the loss of privacy involved. Patients with this symptom may feel that strangers know everything they are thinking. This delusion is also a Schneiderian first rank symptom.

Clinical examples
'People next door seem to know what I'm thinking.'
'It's like phoning to someone. I would think something and they would say it out loud.'
'Whatever a man thinks there is always someone outside who can overhear his thinking.'
'One thought of mine goes into everyone's mind.'

3 Experience of thoughts spoken aloud

This is sometimes known by the German term *gedankenlautwerden,* and refers to the patient's experience that his thoughts are spoken aloud inside his mind. It feels *as if* his thoughts are audible to other people, although the patient knows they are not. If he believes that other people actually can hear his thoughts, then this is classified as a delusion of thought broadcast. The experience of hearing one's own thoughts aloud is another of Schneider's first rank symptoms.

Clinical examples
'When I'm reading a book it seems that people inside can hear my thoughts.'
'I hear my own views.'

4 Experience of thought echo

This is sometimes known by the French term *écho de pensées*. The patient has a thought and immediately afterwards experiences the thought repeated involuntarily. The repetition is in the form of a thought and not a voice. This is another of Schneider's first rank symptoms.

Clinical examples
'Thoughts repeat themselves over and over again like a hurdy-gurdy machine.'
'I think something and then it rethinks it for me.'
'The thought comes back and seems to think the same thing again.'

5 Delusion of thought withdrawal

The patient experiences a sudden interruption in his train of thought. This occurs without warning and is out of the patient's control. For a moment his mind is left completely empty of all thoughts. This distinguishes the symptom from difficulties in concentration which many neurotic patients experience and which they often bring up in response to questions about thought withdrawal. However, these neurotic patients, when pressed, describe one train of thought being interrupted and replaced by another train of thought. This happens involuntarily and even, in the case of obsessional symptoms, against the patient's resistance. But the patient's mind is never left completely empty of thoughts. Only if the patient clearly describes this blankness of mind is the experience of thought block present. If he then goes on to explain his experience in terms of the thoughts being taken out of his mind by some means or other, a delusion of thought withdrawal is present. This is also a Schneiderian first rank symptom.

Clinical examples
1   Thought block
'My thoughts were disappearing.'
'A complete mental blockout, like going into a dark room.'
'My mind goes blank; just ticks over.'
'It's like my thoughts were standing still.'
2   Thought withdrawal
'It feels as if my thoughts had been taken away and cottonwool put in their place.'
'My mind is turned off. Somebody else has got my thoughts.'
'My sister was removing my thoughts by scraping my brain.'

Delusions of control

We normally experience our intentions, our desires, our emotions, and the control of our bodily movements to be part-and-parcel of our own mental activity. Even if our emotions or our desires sometimes seem to be 'out of control', we still recognise them as arising from within ourselves. In the group of symptoms included in delusions of control the patient experiences some outside force or power as replacing, partly or wholly, his control over one or more of these mental activities. The essence of these symptoms is the patient's experience of an alien power from outside himself which forcibly takes over from him. A suitable screening question is: 'Is any force or power other than yourself trying to take control over you?'

Patients with a number of conditions other than delusions of control may answer 'yes' to this question. It is important to differentiate these from delusions of control as the latter constitute another of Schneider's first rank symptoms. Experiences that may be mistaken for delusions of control are as follows:
1   There is a widespread belief among normal people that

everyone's life is planned and directed by a superior power; God or Fate. This belief entails the assumption that each person makes his own decisions, but that they are either endorsed or counter-manded by a higher power. There is no suggestion in this fatalistic or deterministic view of life that an individual's will is replaced or supplanted by any superior power.

2   It is not uncommon for a neurotic patient to assert that when he behaved in a certain way 'I was not myself'. This refers to aspects of his behaviour that he dislikes or rejects. Nevertheless, when pressed, such patients will agree that the behaviour in ques-tion does arise from some part of their own mind, albeit the uncon-scious. Particular difficulty may be posed by patients with obses-sional symptoms. These patients often reject unpleasant thoughts and impulses as not being of their own making and actively resist them. However, they never locate the source of these thoughts and impulses as being outside themselves.

3   Manic patients sometimes express the belief that a greater power has entered into them, usually from God. This power from outside increases their control over the world and their abilities, but always by *adding to* their own will, never by replacing it. These patients invariably experience an *increased* sense of control, not a diminished one.

4   Patients who hear voices giving them orders may or may not obey. Even if they do obey the commands, this does not amount to a delusion of control. The patient's will is not supplanted and he is free to decide whether or not to do what the voices command.

5   Possession states are common in non-Western cultures. They involve the belief that the possessed person is taken over by a supernatural being or spirit, which causes him to behave in an unusual way; forecasting the future, divining the causes of illness or misfortune in others, speaking with different voices, or uttering incomprehensible words. All these features are attributed by the possessed person *and by his cultural group* to the spirit inhabiting him. The facts that possession states are shortlived (several hours at most), occur in the setting of established rituals, and are sanc-tioned by the person's cultural group, distinguish them from delu-

sions of control. It should be noted that possession states were common in England up to three hundred years ago, and that they still form part of the ritual of certain revivalist sects, to which many West Indian immigrants belong. For example, 'speaking in tongues' is sanctioned by the Pentecostals.

The true symptom of delusion of control may be manifested as a belief that the patient's will has been replaced by some power, that parts of his body are moved for him as though he were a puppet or a robot, that someone uses his voice to speak with, or that he is made to want things he would not desire himself. If the interviewer suspects the symptom may be present, he should ask specifically about each of these possible manifestations.

Clinical examples

'People possess my brain and use my mental functions.'

'I feel like a computer, like I've been programmed.'

'They control your arms and legs through your brain.'

'Someone makes my ears move up and down and tries to speak with my voice.'

'The force moved my lips. I began to speak. The words were made for me.'

'Someone switches me on and switches me off.'

'Electrical impulses from the powers of evil control my day-to-day actions.'

'While I was eating food it would fall to the floor. Someone was taking my body over.'

Delusional perception

This symptom is included here because it is one that Schneider designated as first rank, but it is extremely rare to get a clear account from a patient that fits Schneider's description. The symptom consists of two stages; first the patient focuses on a particular percept, and then he suddenly realises that the percept has immense personal significance for him. The link made by the patient between the initial perception and its significance is not understandable or logical to anyone else. We have previously invoked understandability as a method of distinguishing between different forms of speech disorder. Clearly there is a considerable degree of subjectivity involved in this judgement. However in these instances an appeal to the logical thinking of the 'common man' is unavoidable.

The attribution of idiosyncratic meaning to a percept must be distinguished from the common tendency for patients to incorporate perceptions into an already existing delusional system. For example, the patient who believed for some time that he was being spied on and, seeing men working on his neighbour's roof, realised that they were installing microphones. This is *not* a delusional perception because the percept followed the delusion in time and fitted in with it in an understandable way. A suitable screening question is: 'Did you at any time suddenly realise that things held a special meaning for you?'

Clinical examples

A man was asked how many lumps of sugar he wanted in his tea and suddenly understood that the question meant he was king of the universe.

A man standing on a railway platform noticed the British Rail insignia of two arrows pointing in opposite directions. He immediately realised that this meant 'Go to hospital'.

A man was flying in an aeroplane when a ray of light from the setting sun shone through the window next to him. He immediately interpreted this as a sign that he had to preach vegetarianism to the world.

Paranoid delusions

These are the commonest type of delusion and may occur in any of the functional or organic psychoses or may exist as an isolated symptom. The patient believes that a person, a group of people, or some supernatural force is intent on harming him when there is no basis for this in reality. It is essential for the interviewer to assess how realistic the patient's fears are, particularly when a group of people is cited, as there are few societies that are completely free of persecution. An example of the mistakes that can be made is provided by the patient who came to a psychiatric hospital in a state of great anxiety asserting that he was being pursued by a gang of criminals who were intent on torturing him. He was assessed as having paranoid delusions, but his fears were later found to be completely realistic and the gang was eventually brought to justice.

Another source of confusion arises when the patient comes from a culture in which paranoid beliefs are the prevailing mode of thought. For example, in many African rural societies any failure of personal ambition or of crops, or any unwanted occurrence, such as illness or death, tends to be ascribed to witchcraft by envious enemies. Even in societies with a relatively high level of education, such as Greece, belief in the 'evil eye' is widespread and can be found amongst otherwise sophisticated people, who take precautions against others who may actively wish them harm.

True paranoid delusions may be expressed in an unformulated way, for example, the patient who believes that someone or something is trying to harm him but cannot specify who or what. Or they may form a widespread and integrated system in which the patient incorporates each of his experiences, and which is logical and convincing once one accepts the initial premise that he really is being persecuted. He may identify the neighbours as his persecutors, groups such as the Mafia or the FBI, or supernatural beings such as the Devil. A suitable screening question is: 'Is any person, any group of people, or any force trying to harm you?'

Clinical examples
'The Devil is trying to harm my children.'
'I was made into a scapegoat, a whipping boy, by the Labour party.'
'Some cult to do with my dead mother is trying to frighten me out of my flat.'
'A friend of my sister put poison in the rice and peas.'
'I am the target of a lot of criminals who want to kill me.'

59

'I was given cigarettes which contain opium.'
'People at work are victimising me. A bloke at work is trying to kill me with some kind of hypnosis.'

Delusions of reference

The patient sees references to himself in communications which in reality could not possibly be meant for him. The communications may be chance remarks between strangers that he overhears, headlines in the newspapers, comments on the radio or television, advertisements in shop windows, or even street names. They do not have to be in the form of words, but may be non-verbal, as with gestures to which the patient may attribute a personal meaning, or even the colour or arrangement of objects, in which the patient may see a hidden message for himself. The messages that the patient reads into these situations may be pleasant, unpleasant or neutral. For example, he may believe that everyone is passing pleasant remarks about him or that people exchange malicious gossip about him. As with other delusions, this symptom may be expressed in a relatively unformulated way; for example, the patient says he is sure people are talking about him but has no idea what they are saying. In this form, the symptom must be differentiated from simple self-consciousness or ideas of reference. In the latter, the patient feels *as if* everyone is staring at him or talking about him, but is aware that the feeling is due to his sensitivity and that it is not really true.

Some patients report overhearing remarks made by strangers which are addressed directly to them. For example, a woman who was very self-conscious about her small breasts, heard strangers in shops saying, 'You freak'. This symptom must be distinguished from auditory hallucinations, which often occur when the patient is alone, and are rarely attributed by him to actual people in his vicinity. If the patient hears remarks addressed to him only when other people are present and attributes the remarks to them, he has a delusion of reference and *not* auditory hallucinations.

Several screening questions are needed to cover this area: 'Do some people, who may even be strangers, talk about you?'; 'Is there any reference to you in the newspapers, or on radio or television?'; 'Do you see any special meaning for yourself in the colours of objects or the way things are arranged?'

Clinical examples
A patient believed that actors on television were enacting scenes from his own life. A patient in the Maudsley Hospital said that the initials MH on the cutlery stood for 'my highness'. Another patient saw someone scratching his chin and believed it was meant to indicate that the patient needed a shave.
'There is a red light at the gate, which is a warning to stop worrying.'

Delusions of misidentification and misinterpretation

The patient holds mistaken beliefs about the identity of people or places, or misinterprets the nature of situations. He may believe that the nurses are all spies or plainclothes policemen, or that the hospital is really a prison. Occasionally patients express the belief that their close relatives have been replaced by imposters who look identical. This is known as Capgras Syndrome. In relation to situations, the patient may believe that he is being used as a guinea pig in some scientific experiment, or that he is undergoing an endurance test to try out his worth. In the sense that the patient sees himself as the centre of attention, this symptom is closely related to delusions of reference. Indeed the commonly expressed belief that the patient is being closely observed or spied on may be classified as a delusion of reference or of misinterpretation depending on the particular way the patient elaborates on it.

Several screening questions are necessary to probe for these symptoms: 'Are there people around who are not what they seem to be?'; 'Do you ever feel that the place you are in is not what it seems to be?'; 'Is anyone keeping a special watch on you?'; 'Do you feel you are being tested out in some way?'

Clinical examples
'The doctor is the Devil in disguise.'
'There are angels around disguised as people.'
A patient thought the hospital was a space ship.
'All England keeps an eye on me.'
'Recording apparatus in the light sends information about me to a computer.'
'Everybody in the hospital is undergoing an experiment.'

Grandiose delusions

These occur typically in mania, but are also found in schizophrenia and the organic psychoses. There may also be a grandiose element in the delusions associated with depressive psychosis, for example, the patient's conviction that he has brought disaster to the whole world. Grandiose delusions can take a variety of forms. The patient may believe that everyone around him is trying to help him: the reverse of a paranoid delusion. He may assert that he is extremely wealthy, or possessed of exceptional talents or extraordinary powers, often the power of healing. He may express the belief that he is either famous himself or else related to someone famous or to royalty, or even that he is the ruler of the world. Sometimes grandiose delusions take a religious form, the patient maintaining that he has a special mission, that he is Christ or that he receives power directly from God. This latter symptom must be distinguished from a delusion of control (see p. 55). Suitable screening questions are: 'Do you believe anyone is helping you in a special way?'; 'Do you have any special talents or powers out of the ordinary?'; 'Are you a famous person or related to someone famous?'

Clinical examples
'I am the richest man in the world.'
'They use me to boost the World Bank.'
'I have a mission to become a priest. I can make sick people better by my will and thoughts.'

'I can influence the weather. If I feel miserable the weather is miserable.'
'I am a genius in science, arts and sociology.'
'The doctors think I am superintelligent. I have made a discovery about quantum mechanics. Einstein was wrong. E = pke.'
'Give me too much power, I might destroy the world one day.'

Delusions of guilt (or pathological guilt)

These are characteristic of depressive psychosis. Depressed patients commonly express guilt about things they have done in the past. If it is moderately exaggerated it is labelled as pathological (see p. 83), but to be assessed as delusional it has to be out of all proportion to the patient's acts. There are usually three components to delusions of guilt: the patient exaggerates the nature of his bad deeds, he believes he has done a disproportionate amount of harm to the people he loves, and he anticipates some terrible punishment which he feels he deserves. Thus a patient may feel he is the most evil man in the world, that he has ruined his family, and that he will be killed as a punishment. Delusions of guilt may take a religious form, the patient maintaining that he has committed an unpardonable sin and that he will be damned for eternity. Suitable screening questions are: 'Do you feel you have committed a crime or sin?'; 'Have you harmed your family or anyone else?'; 'Do you deserve punishment?'

Clinical examples
'I have committed a terrible sin. Not facing up to life. I must be destroyed. It's pointless going on like this.'
'I have ruined the lives of my family. Being in hospital is a punishment.'
'I had sex. It's a mortal sin. I deserve to be killed.'
'I'm only heartbroken for my father and mother on account of the sins I've committed.'
'I'm disgracing the country.'

Hypochondriacal delusions

These also occur characteristically in depressive psychosis but may be manifested as an isolated symptom. Worry about one's physical health is common in a variety of psychiatric conditions including the neuroses, but for the symptom to be assessed as a delusion the patient must be convinced in the face of contrary evidence that he has some terrible disease. Hypochondriacal delusions commonly involve cancer or venereal disease. Some patients do not specify a particular disease but are convinced that part of their body is rotting away. A concern with the bowels is common amongst the elderly and may take the form of a delusion that their bowels are completely stopped up. A suitable screening question is: 'Are you suffering from any serious disease, or is any part of your body unhealthy?'

Clinical examples:
'I have got cancer of the heart.'
'I haven't had a bowel motion for years. People can smell my insides rotting.'

Nihilistic delusions

These are rare but when they do occur tend to be seen in the setting of depressive psychosis. They involve beliefs either that the patient himself or part of his body do not exist, or else that the world has disappeared or is about to be destroyed. Some patients feel *as if* their brain has been removed, but this is not a nihilistic delusion. The patient has to express the conviction that his skull is empty for this to be regarded as delusional. Suitable screening questions are: 'Do you ever feel that you do not exist?'; 'Is something terrible about to happen?'

Clinical examples
'My brain isn't working at all. My mind has just gone dead. I'm like a walking zombie.'

'My brain has gone like an old man's.'
'When I die the whole world will die.'
'The end of the world is near.'

Religious delusions

These raise particular problems of differentiation from subcultural beliefs. Some beliefs are obviously delusional; that the patient is God, the Virgin Mary, Christ, or a saint. But others, such as the patient's conviction that he has a special relationship with God or that God communicates with him, can be hard to distinguish from beliefs current in minority religious groups to which he may belong. Direct communications from God in the form of inserted thoughts or voices are clearly pathological, whereas indirect communications, as in prayers being answered, are almost certainly normal. A strong sense of a religious mission is particularly difficult to label as pathological with certainty, unless expressed in an extreme form, such as the belief that the patient is meant to save the world. As mentioned earlier, 'speaking in tongues' in which the subject utters nonsensical words, is an acceptable manifestation in certain religious sects, as is possession by God or spirits. The interviewer may be able to resolve doubts about the nature of any of the patient's religious beliefs by asking someone with the same religious affiliation to comment on them. Suitable screening questions are: 'Are you specially holy, perhaps even a saint?'; 'Are you specially close to God?'; 'Does he communicate with you?'

Clinical examples
'I was chosen to be Christ because I am the son of a carpenter and I was born on Good Friday.'
'I must save all. I am the saviour.'
'God and I think on the same frequency.'
'I have been sent to earth by God to gather together all social workers.'
'A pigeon was the Holy Ghost keeping watch over me.'

Sexual delusions

These occur in three forms: as delusions of infidelity, as amorous delusions, and as delusional explanations of hallucinatory experiences of a sexual nature. The former two often occur as isolated symptoms.

Delusions of infidelity, often known as *morbid jealousy,* are an intense form of normal jealousy so that the line between the two is sometimes hard to draw. It is particularly important to get an independent account, that is from someone other than the patient and spouse, as the unfaithful partner may well conceal the truth. Apart from determining whether or not infidelity is really occurring, some clues as to the nature of the patient's belief may be obtained from his behaviour. Close questioning of the spouse as to where she's been and to whom she has talked, searches through her belongings, scrutiny of her clothing for signs of lovemaking, and assessment of her sexual responsiveness as an indication of another source of sexual satisfaction, are all indications that jealousy has reached a morbid level.

Amorous delusions are usually shown by women, who fall in love with some person they know only slightly, and falsely believe that their passion is reciprocated. The object of their passion is often someone who has helped them professionally, such as their doctor or priest. The patient continually makes phone calls, writes letters and loiters about her supposed lover's home in attempts to get close to him.

Sexual delusions may be formed to explain hallucinatory sexual experiences, so that the patient who experiences intercourse when alone may ascribe it to a spirit or to some form of remote control.

Suitable screening questions are: 'Are you particularly jealous of anyone?'; 'Have you experienced any unusual sexual feelings lately?'

Clinical examples
'The two halves of my body make love to each other.'
'The doctors made me pregnant by shooting fucks into me.'

'I am changing into a woman.'
'They made a homosexual attack on me by blowing wind up my back passage.'

Delusional mood

This is a state of mind in which the patient believes that the world about him has changed in some unusual way, but he can't really find an explanation for it. Initially he may feel that he is at the centre of some happening out of the ordinary, but has no idea what it might be. At a later stage in the development of the experience he may be willing to consider a number of possible explanations but has not settled on any particular delusion. The patient is on the threshold of delusional beliefs but may not actually cross it. This state may be a very transient one in the development of a full-blown psychosis, or may last for several days or even weeks and then resolve. Delusional mood is often accompanied by perplexity (see p. 38). A suitable screening question is: 'Does the world about you seem to have changed in some way you can't quite explain?'

Clinical examples
'I look at things and wonder, is that directed at me.'
'All things look different, all places look strange to me. I don't know what is going on.'
'It's like being in a theatre and being part of something, but I don't know what it is.'
'There's something very odd going on out there.'

Hallucinations

A hallucination is a sensory experience lacking sufficient basis in external stimuli, the origin of which the patient nevertheless locates outside of himself. The patient has no appreciation of the lack of an adequate external basis for the perception. Hallucinations may occur in clear consciousness and are then indicative of the presence of a functional psychosis: these kinds form the subject of this chapter. Hallucinations may also occur in states of altered consciousness: these kinds are discussed in Chapter Eight. Hallucinations occur in any of the sensory modalities—vision, hearing, taste, smell and touch, including bodily sensations. They should be distinguished from pseudohallucinations which may fulfil all but one of the criteria for hallucinations. For example, many people who have suffered a bereavement 'see' or 'feel' the dead person. He is often seen sitting in a characteristic attitude in his favourite chair. The hallucination has all the properties of a real perception and is taken to be one by the subject for a second or two, until she remembers that the person is dead. The image immediately vanishes as the subject regains insight. The fact that insight into the unreality of the perception is retained, except for a few seconds, distinguishes this bereavement phenomenon from a true hallucination and marks it out as a *pseudohallucination.* Another example of a pseudohallucination is provided by the person who reports hearing the voices of other people in his mind. The voices have all the qualities of a real auditory perception except that they are located *inside* the subject's mind and not in the external world. Some patients show a progressive exteriorisation of auditory hallucinations in the course of development of their illness, or the reverse process during recovery. True and pseudohallucinations in the same sensory modality can coexist in a single patient. Hypnagogic hallucinations, which occur when the subject is between sleeping and waking, are best classed with pseudohallucinations.

Hallucinations also need to be distinguished from *illusions*. *These are perceptions which are firmly based on an external stimulus, but are a misinterpretation of it.* They often occur in a state of heightened emotion, for example, the person who is walking down a street alone at night, feels somewhat frightened, and mistakes a shadow for a human figure. Unlike delusional perception (p. 57), either insight returns when the emotional state subsides or, if in the setting of a confusional state (p. 94), there may be no recollection of the misinterpretation.

TYPES OF HALLUCINATIONS

Auditory hallucinations

These may occur in any of the functional psychoses, but differ in quality according to whether they form part of a schizophrenic, depressive or manic illness. Therefore, if the patient answers 'yes' to the screening question: 'Do you hear voices when there is nobody there?', further detailed questions are necessary to establish the nature of the experience.

The simplest type of auditory hallucination is hearing one's name called. The person involved looks round to see who has called him but there is no-one there. This is a common occurrence in normal people and should not be counted as pathological, even if it is described by a patient. There are several types of pathological auditory hallucinations.

1 Non-verbal auditory hallucinations

Some patients report hearing clicking or tapping noises or music for which they believe there is some abnormal explanation. It is often hard to tell whether the noises are really occurring and are being misinterpreted by the patient, or whether they constitute true hallucinations. Sometimes, however, it is clear that the patient is hallucinating noises or music. This symptom has no diagnostic significance other than indicating the presence of a psychosis.

Clinical examples
A patient reported hearing music and the singing of choirs. Another patient heard humming when there was no-one present. Another patient heard birds singing and applause. A patient reported hearing people sharpening knives outside the window.

2 Verbal auditory hallucinations

These can occur in the form of muttering or whispering. This may be a stage in the development or disappearance of clearly heard voices, or may be all that the patient ever hears. In the latter case, if the patient cannot make out the words, the symptom is useless for distinguishing between the major functional psychoses. Only if the patient hears the voice or voices clearly and gives examples of what is said, can such diagnostic distinctions be made.

Confusion sometimes arises between auditory hallucinations and *delusions of reference* (see p. 60). Some patients report hearing voices making remarks about them but always assert that they come from people who are present at the time. This is a delusion of reference and *not* an auditory hallucination. The phenomenon can only be classed as an auditory hallucination when the patient believes that what he hears comes from somewhere other than people in his presence.

2A Third person auditory hallucinations*

A voice or voices discuss the patient in the third person referring to the patient as he or she. The experience is like overhearing a conversation about yourself between two or more people who are

---

*In grammar, the first person is *I*, the second person is *you* and the third person is *he*, *she* or *it*.

unaware that you are listening in. Another variant of this symptom is hearing a voice or voices giving a running commentary on what the patient is doing, reading, or thinking. Both types of auditory hallucination are Schneiderian first rank symptoms. Despite the implication that third person auditory hallucinations are diagnostic of schizophrenia, they may occasionally occur in patients with otherwise characteristic manic or depressive illnesses. In these instances, they take the form of isolated brief phrases, such as 'He's the greatest' or 'she must die'.

Clinical examples
'Here comes that look again. Why is he using his hands. He's going to ECT in the morning.'
'She is reading. She's sitting down. She's radioactive.'
'He wants a girl. He wants to be a singer. He's picking up a glass now.'
'She's disgusting. She can do better than that.'

2B   Second person auditory hallucinations

A voice or voices talk to the patient directly and address the patient as you. For diagnostic purposes it is essential to relate this symptom to the patient's prevailing affect. This is determined from non-verbal (see Chapter Four) and verbal (see Chapter Seven) information. The content of the hallucinations may be pleasant, unpleasant or neutral. If it is pleasant and the prevailing affect is manic or hypomanic then the likely diagnosis is mania. If the content is unpleasant or derogatory and the prevailing affect is depressive, then the likely diagnosis is depressive psychosis. Patients with this condition will say that they deserve the unpleasant remarks they hear. If the patient shows blunted affect regardless of the content of the hallucinations, or if the prevailing affect is markedly incongruous with their content, the diagnosis is likely to be schizophrenia.

Clinical examples
1   Auditory hallucinations in combination with euphoric mood.

'You are God's representative. You have been chosen.'

'You shouldn't be in hospital. Go out and save the world.'

'Allah is the greatest. Ali take off everything. Ali you are my servant. You are my chosen one.'

'Rosy, you are my posy, the nicest one of all.'

2   Auditory hallucinations in combination with depressed mood.

'You've let them all down.'

'You're being childish. You're a nasty, lazy man.'

'You ought to be ashamed of yourself.'

3   Auditory hallucinations in combination with blunted affect.

'Sweep the floor. Have a shower. Shut up.'

'A pint of milk keeps the doctor away. Safety first.'

'Take off your jacket. Carry on, John.'

'Pack up. Don't pack up. You'll be sorry for this.'

'Throw yourself out of the window and people will think it's a miracle.'

Visual hallucinations

Like auditory hallucinations, visual hallucinations can occur in any of the functional psychoses so that their presence does not automatically indicate a particular diagnosis. A suitable screening question is: 'Do you see visions, or things that other people can't see?' The word 'vision' is used because true visual hallucinations are much rarer than true auditory hallucinations. Patients with abnormal visual perceptions usually interpret them as visions, that is a special experience often granted by God or some other spiritual power. They rarely believe that they have seen real people or objects. To be mistaken for reality, visual hallucinations need to move, to be coloured, and to be experienced as 3-dimensional. They often lack one or more of these qualities. If they are static, black and white, and flat they are best categorized as visual pseudohallucinations (see p. 69).

As discussed above, visual hallucinations have to be distinguished from illusions and hypnagogic experiences. If a diagnosis of functional psychosis is being considered, it is also important to determine whether the level of consciousness is altered at the time of the visual experiences (see Chapter Eight). The content of visual hallucinations is not important diagnostically, although it tends to be consistent with mood. Thus the euphoric patient sees visions of God and the saints, while the depressed patient is tormented by images of corpses and the damned.

Clinical examples

A patient saw a hand beckoning in the sky. Another patient saw himself on the crucifix as Christ. Another patient had visions of angels. Another patient reported seeing Isaiah, Jesus and Mohammed sitting together outside the window.

Gustatory hallucinations

Patients unused to institutional cooking will often complain that hospital food tastes peculiar, particularly if they belong to a minority ethnic group with its own dietary and cooking habits. This should not of course be considered pathological. Only if the patient detects some particular and unusual taste in his food should the interviewer consider the possibility of gustatory hallucinations. This possibility is strengthened if the patient has some delusional explanation for the peculiar taste. The interviewer needs to be aware that a number of drugs in medical use affect taste. Patients on tricyclic antidepressants, for example, commonly complain of a nasty taste in the mouth. A suitable screening question is: 'Have you noticed a peculiar taste in your food or drink? What is this due to?'

Clinical examples

'An apple tasted like the smell of the devil.'
'The food tastes like poison.'
'There is a taste of iodine in the coffee and sugar.'

Olfactory hallucinations

As with gustatory hallucinations, it is hard to be certain of the presence of olfactory hallucinations unless the patient complains of a particular and unusual smell. A suitable screening question is: 'Have you noticed any peculiar smell lately? What is it due to?'

Clinical examples
'I can smell putrid smells due to the influence of Satan.'
'My persecutors make unpleasant smells around me.'
'I smell dead flowers; the sort they bring around when people die.'
A patient smelled incense in the ward.

Tactile and somatic hallucinations

Patients experience sensations of touch, heat, cold, vibration, pressure or pain on the surface of the body in the absence of an external stimulus. They may also report unusual feelings inside the body, or feel that they are floating. The attribution of somatic hallucinations to some force acting over a distance is one of Schneider's first rank symptoms. It is known as an experience of bodily influence. Suitable screening questions are: 'Do you feel someone touch you when there is no-one there?'; 'Do you have any unusual feelings in your body? What are they due to?'

Clinical examples
'I feel spirits from the devil touching me and running up and down inside my back.'
'A feeling of thunder and lightning went through my arm.'
'Crawly things run down to my feet.'
'My right arm feels lighter since the doctors drew blood from it.'
'I can feel a lizard moving in my stomach.'
'I have a feeling of floating. It's due to a sugar-free diet.'

Experiences of bodily influence
'They work a machine which makes me feel an electric current passing through me.'

'The landlord has an instrument that penetrates into my internal organs. It gives me a pain in my heart and liver.'
'The double people use an excavator or incavator to break my veins down. It gives me so much pain I don't have any strength left.'

Insight

This refers to the patient's awareness of the abnormality of his experiences. Further than that, the degree of insight measures the extent of the patient's understanding that his symptoms signify the presence of a mental illness. Loss of insight is common in psychotic conditions, and is assessed in part, by the firmness with which the patient holds to his delusional beliefs and by the conviction with which he maintains that his hallucinations have a real origin in the outside world. These features will have been dealt with in the questioning about specific delusions and hallucinations, so that during the process of establishing the presence of these symptoms the interviewer will gain a good idea of the degree of the patient's insight. However, it is worth asking a few more general questions in addition. Partial insight is shown by some patients who deny having a psychiatric condition, but will state that they are physically ill. Suitable screening questions are: 'What do you think is the matter with you?'; 'Do you consider that you are ill in any way?'; 'Is it a mental or physical condition?' If the patient denies any kind of illness, ask: 'Why did you have to come to hospital?'

CHAPTER SEVEN

Neurotic and Affective Symptoms

The main problem in elucidating the presence of psychotic symptoms lies in deciding whether what the patient tells you about his experiences matches the criteria for particular symptoms. By contrast, the main problem with neurotic symptoms is not the nature of the patient's experience, but whether his discomfort reaches an intense enough level to be considered pathological. (For this reason, in contrast to the preceding chapter, clinical examples of symptoms will not be given.) For example, every normal person becomes sad or miserable at times. The psychiatrist has to determine whether this mood is intense or prolonged enough to be considered a depressive symptom. Thus, much of his crossquestioning in this area will concern the intensity and duration of experiences. Furthermore, a distinction often needs to be made between personality characteristics, such as cyclothymia or obsessional traits, and pathological symptoms. This may be difficult as certain aspects of the personality can become intensified when a neurotic illness supervenes. Two clinical examples of the kind of crossquestioning that can be useful follow.

Example 1

Interviewer: Have you felt depressed or low-spirited lately?
Patient: Yes, specially in the last week.
I: How bad has it been?

P: Very bad. I've never felt like this before.

I: Can you manage to enjoy yourself?

P: Well, I used to like going to the pub with the missus, but it's such an effort now, I'd rather not go.

I: How much of the time do you feel miserable?

P: It goes on all day from the moment I open my eyes until I go to bed, and even then I don't sleep like I used to.

Comment: This patient describes a clear onset of a depressive mood change of considerable severity. There is no doubt from his description of its pathological nature.

Example 2

Interviewer: Have you felt depressed or low-spirited lately?

Patient: Yes, I've always been moody.

I: Has it been any worse recently?

P: No, I don't think so.

I: What sort of things make you depressed?

P: If someone says something nasty at work, it'll spoil the whole day for me. I've always been easily upset.

I: Can you enjoy yourself?

P: Oh yes, if I'm with my friends. We go out and have a good time.

I: Have you been crying much lately?

P: Only when I listen to records.

I: What sort of records?

P: You know, sad ones about unhappy lovers. That sort of thing.

Comment: This patient describes personality traits of moodiness and sensitivity. She gives no evidence of a recent onset of depressive symptoms. Her crying in response to the records is indicative of sentimentality, not depression.

There are a number of key neurotic symptoms which will be dealt with in this chapter, such as depression, anxiety and obsessions. Each of these symptoms is commonly associated with a cluster of other symptoms, together making up a syndrome. Every component of a syndrome is not always present, but a knowledge of the common associations enables the interviewer to ask the relevant subsidiary questions once he has established the presence of the key symptom.

As in other textbooks, the symptoms of anxiety and depression are here described as distinct entities. It must be recognised, however, that in practice, many patients present a combination of the two and that they are commonly difficult to disentangle from the patient's account. Furthermore, the organisation of certain symptoms into syndromes has been done largely for convenience of presentation and is not meant to imply invariable clinical associations. For this reason, even if the key symptom in a syndrome is absent, the secondary symptoms should be inquired about.

DEPRESSION

The central symptom here is of course depressed mood, but it is possible for a patient to be suffering from a depressive condition without complaining of depressed mood either spontaneously or on careful questioning. Patients of this type commonly focus on somatic symptoms and seem to be unaware of the cognitive aspect of depression. The problems posed by such patients will be discussed in Chapter Nine.

Depressed mood

The problem of distinguishing a depressive mood change from moodiness as a personality trait has already been discussed and illustrated. It is important to assess the depth of the depressed mood, by asking, for example, how much it interferes with the patient's ability to enjoy life. It is useful to establish whether the patient can be cheered up by seeing friends or watching a comedy programme. The patient should also be asked to describe in their own words what it feels like when their mood is at its lowest. The development of crying spells with no apparent precipitant is another indication of the severity of a depressed mood. It must be remembered, however, that women cry more readily than men, and also that some depressions become so severe that the patient is beyond crying. Such patients report that they feel like crying but are quite unable to shed tears, and that to do so would be a relief.

The duration of the depressed mood is another index of its severity: whether it lasts throughout the day or only for short periods; whether it comes on every day or whether the patient feels quite normal for as long as a day at a time. Diurnal variation in mood is important to inquire about, as there is some evidence that it predicts response to particular treatments. The patient may remark spontaneously that he feels worse when he wakes up in the morning, but if not then the relevant question should be asked. Some patients feel depressed throughout the day but experience a lifting of mood in the evening.

Associated symptoms

Insomnia
The patient with depression characteristically wakes early in the morning and can't get back to sleep again. As people vary greatly in their habitual waking time, it is of value to ask the patient what time he usually wakes up, and what time he has been waking recently. Some patients do not show classical early morning waking, but instead wake intermittently throughout the night or else lie awake for a long time, when they first go to bed. For this reason a general screening question should be asked of the form: 'Has your sleep been disturbed recently?' It must be remembered that insomnia is very likely to be treated symptomatically by the patient's general practitioner. Therefore, it is necessary to ask if any night sedation has been prescribed and if so what the patient's sleep was like beforehand.

Anorexia
Many patients with depression lose their appetite and this can lead to quite a substantial weight loss. Some patients do not lose their taste for food but nevertheless lose weight, so that questions should be asked both about loss of appetite and loss of weight. Not every person weighs himself regularly so that weight loss can occur unsuspected by the patient. If the interviewer thinks this is the case he should ask the patient what his usual weight is and then arrange to have him weighed.

Loss of libido
Loss of interest in sex is another common accompaniment of depressed mood. In our culture the man usually initiates intercourse, so that depression in men may result in a reduction in the frequency of intercourse. Erectile impotence may also develop and on occasions is the presenting symptom of a depressive illness. Depressed women may comply with intercourse at the usual frequency, but commonly lose their enjoyment of it. Therefore, both frequency and enjoyment of intercourse need to be inquired about. Because they both vary enormously from person-to-person, the interviewer should ask about any change in the patient's usual pattern. This can be an embarrassing area for both patient and interviewer and needs to be approached tactfully. If questions on sexual interest are asked in the context of other vegetative functions such as sleep and appetite there is usually no difficulty.

Loss of interest
Depressed patients often lose interest in activities that they normally value and enjoy. This may affect work, housework, leisure activities, hobbies and care for one's personal appearance. All these areas should be inquired about.

Impaired concentration
The patient finds it difficult to keep his mind on what he should be thinking about. His thoughts drift off when he tries to read, watch television, carry out his job, or follow what people are saying. He

may be aware of a slowing down of his thought processes, which makes it more difficult to come to a decision about anything. This symptom needs to be distinguished from obsessional hesitations (see p. 109) which also interfere with the making of decisions.

Exhaustion

It is common for depressed patients to complain of lack of energy. Indeed it may be the dominant symptom. It is often associated with a slowing down of movements, which is another feature of depression. Exhaustion may show the same diurnal variation as depressed mood itself, the patient waking in the morning with the feeling that he has no energy to tackle any task and gradually recovering as the day wears on. A specific inquiry should be made if the patient does not mention exhaustion spontaneously.

Hopelessness

The gloom of depression may express itself as a loss of hope in the future. The patient may feel that the future is bound to be unpleasant, or in extreme cases that there is no future for him at all. Feelings of hopelessness are sometimes focused on the illness itself, giving rise to the belief that treatment will be of no help and that the patient will never recover. It is important to ask about feelings of hopelessness as they are closely related to suicidal intent.

Suicidal intent

It is of prime importance to determine how intense the patient's suicidal feelings are, because suicide is now virtually the only cause of death in non-organic psychiatric conditions and is potentially preventable. The interviewer should not hesitate to inquire about suicidal intent in any psychiatric patient, whatever the presumptive diagnosis. In its mildest form this symptom appears as a feeling that life is not worth living, without any thoughts of killing oneself. The next stage in severity is the belief that one would be better off dead, without any consideration of the means of suicide. Once the patient has contemplated a particular way or ways of killing himself the symptom is well established and must be treated seriously. Of course some patients may actually have made a suicide attempt, or several attempts. These should be gone into in considerable detail and an assessment made of the danger to the patient's life. Hanging, drowning and shooting are indicative of a determination to die, whereas the intent behind the taking of pills varies considerably. The interviewer should ask about the nature of the pills swallowed, the number taken, and the likelihood of the patient being found in time for treatment to be given. The actual treatment received should also be determined as it is a useful index of the severity of the attempt.

Low self-esteem

A poor opinion of oneself is common as part of the depressive picture. In some patients this develops along with the depression, while in others it is a longstanding personality trait which antedates the illness and may in fact contribute to its cause. The extreme form of this symptom is shown by patients who assert that they are completely worthless. The interviewer should ask if the patient feels as good as other people or any worse, and if this is a recent feeling or whether he has always felt somewhat inferior.

Guilt

In the severe forms of depression, the patient may blame himself unnecessarily for things he has done or has failed to do in the past. Of course the guilt is only pathological if these acts or omissions are trivial in nature. Acts about which the depressed patient feels guilty commonly have a sexual connotation. Some patients focus their guilt on the present rather than the past, and blame themselves for becoming ill and for their inability to 'pull themselves together'. As this symptom increases in severity it takes on a delusional character, so that it may be difficult to draw a hard and fast line between neurotic guilt and delusions of guilt (see p. 63).

Apart from blaming themselves, some patients feel that they are blamed by other people. If the patient accepts this blame and considers it to be deserved, he is suffering from severe guilt. If, however, he believes that he is quite guiltless and is being unjustly blamed, he is likely to hold paranoid delusions, which should then be inquired about.

Hypochondriasis

An excessive concern with the possibility of bodily illness may occur as part of the depressive syndrome or may present as an isolated symptom, which some people view as a depressive equivalent. A mild concern with bodily health is understandable in someone who is talking to a doctor, but if it keeps intruding during the interview while other topics are being discussed, it should be considered pathological, particularly when there is no objective justification for the concern expressed. Patients are usually concerned about cancer or heart disease. Some patients focus on their autonomic symptoms, such as palpitations or faintness, which they interpret as indications of heart disease. This makes them more anxious and completes a vicious circle. Patients with hypochondriasis can usually be reassured for a short while, but invariably return to their preoccupation. If reassurance by the doctor fails to give even temporary relief, the patient is likely to be suffering from hypochondriacal delusions (see p. 64).

ANXIETY

Anxious mood is central to this syndrome, but as with depression some patients do not complain of it directly. Instead they present a variety of somatic complaints which the interviewer may be able to identify as part of the anxiety syndrome. This particular problem is dealt with in Chapter Nine.

Anxious mood

The essence of anxiety is that it is an unreasonable fear without any particular focus. If the fearfulness is focused on an object or situation it is classified as a phobia, which will be discussed separately. In contrast to phobias, there is no obvious and *immediate* cause for general anxiety, although a causal connection with the patient's life circumstances may be traced. As with depression, the interviewer's task is to distinguish pathological anxiety from the mild anxiety that affects most normal people from time-to-time. It is normal, for example, to feel mildly anxious just before an examination. A minor degree of anxiety is in fact a spur to better performance. If, however, the anxiety becomes severe enough to impair the person's performance, then it can be assessed as pathological. The patient should therefore be asked how much the anxiety interferes with his everyday life. Bouts of anxiety that come on suddenly while the person is carrying out routine tasks should also be judged as pathological. Apart from the abruptness and severity of the anxiety attacks, the patient should be asked about their duration. Do they last for a few minutes at a time or for as much as an hour? Do they come on every day and how many times in a particular day?

The occasional patient never suffers from anxiety during the day but only gets attacks at night. In this pattern, the patient wakes from sleep and feels that he is going to die, with the fear that his heart will stop beating or that his breathing will stop.

Attacks of anxiety are often accompanied by a variety of somatic symptoms: palpitations, excessive sweating, breathlessness, faintness, a sinking feeling in the stomach, nausea, shakiness. Most patients have a particular somatic symptom or set of symptoms that they focus on when they experience anxiety. Patients should be asked about the range of possible somatic symptoms if they do not report them spontaneously.

Attacks of anxiety may reach such a peak of severity that the patient gets into a panic. In this state the patient desperately seeks help from any quarter. He may turn to the nearest stranger, try to contact his friends or his doctor, or may actually scream for help. If the interviewer suspects that the patient suffers from anxiety he should inquire about the occurrence of panic attacks as an index of severity.

Apart from episodes of anxiety, the patient may complain of a persistent fear of something terrible happening. As with the attacks, there is no particular focus. The patient is vague about the kind of disaster he is anticipating, but suffers from an unpleasant sense of foreboding. If he believes that there *is* some specific catastrophe about to befall him he is probably suffering from a form of nihilistic delusion (see p. 64).

Phobic anxiety

For this symptom to be judged present, the patient should complain of anxiety which is linked with particular objects or situations. The objects may be animals, such as dogs, cats, birds, spiders, or something inanimate, such as thunder or water. The situations which commonly engender phobic anxiety are open spaces, enclosed spaces, travelling in a vehicle, being left alone, being in crowds, and meeting people. Sometimes it may be difficult to distinguish a travel phobia from a phobia of crowds. Patients should be asked whether they feel easier in an empty bus or train than in a crowded one. Patients with a crowd phobia may cross the road to avoid walking past a bus queue, and are likely to enter a shop only when it is relatively empty. Most patients are well aware of their phobia and have often worked out ways of totally avoiding the feared situation or object. If their strategy is effective they may not have experienced phobic anxiety for years. Therefore, it is necessary for the interviewer to ask the patient if he would feel anxious were he to be faced with particular situations, as well as the more direct question about *overt* phobic anxiety.

An occasional patient who suffers from phobic anxiety remains unaware of the link with particular situations and presents his symptom as general anxiety. It is important to establish the presence of phobic anxiety because of the specific treatments now available. Therefore, every patient who reports general anxiety should be asked where he is and what he is doing at the time of his attacks to determine whether any pattern emerges.

Depersonalisation

This is not a common symptom, but when it occurs tends to be associated with anxiety. The patient experiences a sense of personal unreality. This may affect him totally or only part of his body, so that he feels, for example, that his hands don't belong to him. The patient may express the feeling that he is detached from his own body and looking at it from the outside, or that his reflection in the mirror looks unreal. A suitable screening question is: 'Do you ever have the feeling that you are unreal?'

Derealisation

This is closely related to depersonalisation, but instead of experiencing *himself* as unreal, the patient feels that the world around him is unreal. People and objects seem to be more distant than usual. They may also appear to take on an artificial quality, as though they were two-dimensional figures cut out of cardboard. Sometimes the patient feels as if everyone is acting a part, like being at the theatre. If he really believes that people *are* pretending to be somebody else, he does not exhibit derealisation but holds a delusion of misidentification (see p. 61). A suitable screening question is: 'Do you ever feel that the world around you is unreal?'

Irritability

Increased irritability can occur in any psychiatric illness and is therefore of little diagnostic importance, except in one condition, namely emotionally unstable personality. However, it does affect the management of the patient, particularly when it escalates into violence, so is worth inquiring about. Habitual irritability is characteristic of emotionally unstable personality, but if a symptom is to be judged as present rather than a personality trait, the patient should report an increase in his usual level of irritability. This may be shown by quarrelling, by shouting, by throwing things, by physical violence to people, or by the destruction of objects.

OBSESSIONS

A difficult but important distinction needs to be made in this area between obsessional personality traits and obsessional symptoms. Obsessional traits are relatively common and can be a distinct advantage in a job that demands precision. Obsessional symptoms are relatively rare and are always handicapping either socially or occupationally or both. Symptoms may take the form of *obsessional acts* or *obsessional thoughts*.

Obsessional acts

These are repetitive acts, usually commonplace in nature, which the patient feels compelled to carry out, although he resists them as unnecessary or even stupid. There are a variety of these, comprising checking procedures, obsessional cleanliness, and other rituals. Many normal people check once or twice that they have turned off gas taps, switches and water taps, and that they have closed windows and locked doors. It is only when these procedures become time-consuming or interfere with other activities that they should be considered pathological. For example, someone who has to check taps at least three times, or who has to return to the house to check the front door lock after setting out, is probably exhibiting an obsessional symptom. However, there are other criteria that have to be met, namely that the person *remembers* performing the act, but has to satisfy a lingering doubt that he has done it correctly. The need to recheck actions is also commonly shown by patients with memory problems. The clear memory of the act distinguishes an obsessional symptom from forgetfulness due to preoccupation with other matters or organic amnesia. In addition, the person should feel that it is in reality unnecessary to perform the act again, and hence has some resistance against re-doing it. However, the resistance is overcome by the force of the obsessional doubt. The person's realisation that the act or thought is silly and the accompanying resistance are characteristic features of obsessional symptoms and should always be inquired about. However, it must be noted that patients' resistance to repetitive acts or thoughts decreases over time and may eventually disappear altogether.

An intense preoccupation with cleanliness may be an obsessional symptom. It commonly takes the form of washing or bathing much more frequently than usual. Norms for these activities vary considerably from person to person, but anyone who bathes twice a day or more, or who washes so frequently that their skin becomes red and raw, should be suspected of having an obsessional symptom. In housewives this symptom may present as excessive housecleaning. If sweeping, dusting and cleaning the home are performed more than once a day, or if these chores take up most of the day, even extending into the night, they are almost certainly indicative of pathology. Another form of obsessional cleanliness involves the avoidance of physical contact with people or with objects they have touched, such as door handles, cutlery and crockery. In all cases where the interviewer suspects the obsessional nature of excessive cleanliness he should ask the reason for it. Patients commonly express an intense fear of contamination by dirt, or even of infection by germs.

Some obsessional acts take the form of rituals, such as the compulsion to go on counting numbers, or to touch every lamp-post the person passes. Sometimes rituals become very elaborate and involve the repetition of a variety of acts in exactly the same order each time. They may take up a great deal of the patient's waking hours.

A number of screening questions are necessary to cover obsessional acts: 'Do you have to check things many times even though you know you have done them correctly?'; 'Do you wash very often even though you know you are clean?'; 'Do you have to repeat any actions many times and in exactly the same order?'

Obsessional thoughts

These are unpleasant thoughts, often with a violent, sexual, or distasteful content, which repeatedly force themselves into the patient's mind against his will. They are repetitive in nature and are repellent or even horrifying to the patient, who resists them strongly but unsuccessfully. In some cases the thoughts are stimulated by external perceptions, hence providing the patient with a means of controlling them. For example, obsessional thoughts of harming those the patient loves are commonly brought on by seeing knives. Patients often find that by putting knives out of sight and avoiding looking at them, they can reduce the frequency of their unpleasant thoughts. Patients may develop rituals of thought or action in an attempt to neutralise the unwelcome thoughts.

Obsessional thoughts need to be distinguished from the experience of thought insertion, which is a Schneiderian first rank symptom (see p. 52). There should be no confusion with the *full* delusion, because patients with this symptom identify alien thoughts as arising from *outside* their mind, something which never occurs with obsessional thoughts. The *partial* delusion consists of the experience of alien thoughts which the patient is prepared to consider as products of his unconscious mind. Alienation is also shown by the sufferer from obsessional thoughts who finds them so distasteful that he too rejects them as his own, but will agree that they could arise from his unconscious mind. The distinction between these very similar experiences hinges on the patient's resistance to the thoughts, which is only present in the obsessional symptom.

A suitable screening question is: 'Do unpleasant thoughts keep coming back into your mind even though you struggle against them?'

HYPOMANIA

The central symptom of this syndrome is elevated mood, but there are other symptoms, such as psychomotor overactivity and grandiosity, which are commonly associated with the mood change.

Elevated mood

Most normal people experience periods of cheerfulness or high-spirits without any obvious cause. For the elevation of mood to be assessed as pathological, however, there must be a quality of excitement to it which is quite out of the ordinary, as well as being disproportionate to the patient's circumstances. The patient may be quite unaware of the unnatural quality of his mood. Patients use phrases to describe their mood such as, 'on top of the world', 'never felt better in my life', 'feel like bursting into song'.

A suitable screening question is: 'Do you ever feel excessively cheerful or excited?' Most people will answer 'yes' to this question, so that the interviewer has to be very critical about assessing the quality of the mood change described in response to further crossquestioning.

Psychomotor overactivity

The patient's mental and bodily functions are speeded up, and his appetites are increased. He may report his cognitive over-activity as a feeling that thoughts are flashing through his mind almost too fast for him to keep up with. On the motor side, his movements are faster so that he feels that other people are going too slowly for him. He also has much more energy, sleeps less than usual, and may in fact continue his physical activity right through the night, often tackling one task after another. He talks more volubly and quicker than before and may be aware of this. He experiences an increased appetite for food and for sex, and may develop completely new interests.

Grandiosity

Hypomanic patients often develop an inflated view of their qualities and abilities. This may be expressed as a belief that they are exceptionally intelligent, in superb physical health, carrying out their job with extra efficiency, or capable of pursuing any one of a number of different careers. Grandiosity may also be shown by unusual extravagance with money. Grandiose ideas may of course progress to become delusional (see p. 62). At this point in the illness, hypomania would generally be considered to have developed into mania.

SELF-CONSCIOUSNESS

This is more often a longstanding personality characteristic than an acute symptom. However, the personality trait may be intensified by the development of any psychiatric illness. Self-consciousness appears as an uncomfortable awareness of being stared at, even by strangers. A more intense form of the symptom is the feeling of being laughed at or talked about critically. However, the patient with this symptom can always be reassured and will admit that it is all due to his excessive sensitivity. If he cannot be reassured and is convinced of the reality of the experience, he does not have this symptom but is suffering from a delusion of reference (see p. 60).

CHAPTER EIGHT

Organic Conditions

Those disorders of the central nervous system that are usually classified as psychiatric disabilities are the *acute confusional state* (delirium), the *amnestic syndrome* (or Korsakoff psychosis) and *dementia* (or chronic brain syndrome). Each has characteristic features and can often be diagnosed from the history alone, the mental state examination frequently just providing confirmatory evidence for the diagnosis.

DISORDERS OF HIGHER CEREBRAL FUNCTION

Disorders of higher cerebral function due to localised brain lesions are generally classified as neurological disorders, but on occasions the disturbance of language or movement might be sufficiently severe to suggest a psychiatric condition. In addition, some features of localised cerebral disturbances are frequently found in patients suffering from dementia, eg dressing apraxia and nominal asphasia, anosognosia. Detailed assessment of patients with such difficulties is outside the scope of this book but it is useful to apply some simple screening tests if a localised cerebral lesion is suspected. These should be concerned with *language* and *praxis*.

Language function should be considered in relation to the patient's ability to understand the spoken or written word as well as his ability to express himself, which includes the capacity to name simple objects. Simple tests of comprehension can include observation of the patient's response to simple commands, eg stand up, open your mouth, pick up the pen and so on. If the patient is not able to express himself in speech, comprehension can also be tested by inviting him to reply to questions by gesture, eg 'Do trees have leaves in the winter?'; 'Is it raining at the moment?' The patient's ability to *express* himself in words will be apparent from ordinary conversation, but he should be asked to name a series of simple objects.

Praxis, which is the ability to carry out a purposeful movement sequence, can be tested by asking the patient to make certain simple movements such as shaking hands, waving goodbye, showing how to salute or how to strike a match.

Disturbances of language function (dysphasia) or of praxis (apraxia) arise especially from lesions of the parietal lobe.

If such simple screening suggests the possibility of a localised cerebral lesion a more comprehensive assessment is needed for which various schemes are available (Bickerstaff 1980; Meadows 1975).

ACUTE CONFUSIONAL STATE (DELIRIUM)

The acute confusional state is characterised by *clouding of consciousness, restlessness, disorientation, illusions, visual hallucinations*, with the patient appearing *afraid and perplexed*. As the name implies, it is a condition of recent and sudden onset and a carefully taken history will usually suggest the underlying physical cause.

The use of the term confusion should be restricted to acute or subacute organic conditions and these invariably have some if not all the features described. The term is sometimes, but quite inappropriately used to describe patients whose behaviour is seriously disorganised by other conditions, eg an acute schizophrenic illness or a state of manic excitement. While a lay person might describe such a patient as confused in a general sense, the term should never be used in that way in psychiatry. As indicated above, it should be strictly limited to those conditions that have a clear organic basis.

Clouding of consciousness

A patient can be described as fully conscious if he is completely aware of his surroundings. In the acute confusional state the patient's awareness is diminished so that he seems slightly drowsy, and appears to have only a vague interest in things around him. In this condition the patient will often be seen gazing in a somewhat vacant manner but is easily startled by external stimuli such as a door banging or an unfamiliar person approaching. Such occurrences readily distract from the business of the interview and much patient persuasion will be needed to sustain his attention. A change in the level of consciousness of this nature is known as clouding and is always indicative of an acute organic condition.

Disorientation

Orientation is awareness of oneself in relation to time, place and person, and this awareness is invariably disturbed when a patient is acutely confused. To test the patient's orientation in each of these three spheres a series of routine questions should be asked and ideally the verbatim reply to each recorded with a correct answer given in brackets.

Time orientation
The patient should be asked to state the *day, month* and *year* as well as the time to the nearest hour. Naming the *season* of the year is an additional way of assessing the patient's awareness of himself and relation to time.

Place orientation
This is assessed by asking the patient to say where he is, at present, as well as the nature of the place. It is not unusual for patients to give evasive answers to such questions, eg 'It's a very nice place' or 'I often come here'. Despite such replies the matter must be pursued slowly and patiently to establish how accurately the patient knows where he is at the time. With regard to

the nature of the place suitable questions would be: 'What sort of place is this?'; 'Is this your home?'; 'Is this an hotel?' (for patient in hospital); 'What is this place called?' If the patient is in hospital and has been there for an adequate length of time, he should be asked about the layout of the ward, eg 'Which is the entrance?'; 'Where is the bathroom?'; 'Where is sister's office?' and so on.

Person orientation
The way this is tested will vary with the setting in which the examination is conducted. Thus, should it be in the patient's own home, he should be asked to name close relatives and state their relationship to him. When disorientated a husband might identify his wife as his mother or sister, or even deny being related in any way. In a hospital setting, a patient should be able to recognise a nurse or identify the interviewer as a doctor and realise the status of his fellow patients. Suitable questions in a hospital setting would be: 'Could you tell me who some of these people are in the ward?'; 'What do you think her job is?' (pointing to a nurse); 'Do you recognise anyone here?'; 'What do you think all these people are doing here?'

Illusions (also see p. 70)

An illusion is the false interpretation of a real stimulus. Unlike a delusional perception the misinterpretation is understandable. Thus a ticking clock might be thought to be a time-bomb, or a shadow might be seen as a person. Typically, such experiences are more evident at night, but the patient will often recall them in response to suitable questions, eg 'Has anything frightened you recently?'; 'Have you had any strange experiences at night?'; 'Has anything been puzzling you lately?'

Visual hallucinations (also see p. 73)

These are visual experiences occurring in the absence of an appropriate stimulus, and are one of the most consistent features of the acute confusional state. The patient should be asked whether he has seen anything lately that puzzled him. 'Has anything unusual been going on in this room?'; 'Have you seen anything you didn't quite understand?'; 'Have you seen anything that puzzled you or frightened you?'

As with illusions, visual hallucinations are more common at night when they often have a frightening quality. Thus, patients might describe water cascading down the walls, children playing on the floor, traffic driving through the room. A more dramatic example was given by an elderly patient recovering from influenza who suddenly wished to chop down a nearby tree, as he could see a man sitting on top of it keeping him under constant observation.

Once these characteristic features of the full acute confusional state have been elicited, special investigations are usually required to establish the exact cause, but if the patient is being examined in his own home the opportunity should not be lost to look for possible relevant clues. Thus, finding large numbers of empty spirit bottles will point to alcoholism. There may be drugs that can be toxic if the patient is sensitive, or takes more than the prescribed dose. The presence of decomposing food, an accumulation of unopened milk bottles or simply empty cupboards will raise the possibility of dietary neglect, whereas inadequate heating or damp living conditions would suggest hypothermia as a possible factor. When possible, a physical examination should also be carried out and should include taking the patient's temperature.

AMNESTIC SYNDROME (KORSAKOFF PSYCHOSIS)

A feature of this condition is the patient's lack of awareness or denial of having any disability and includes his attempt to conceal or minimise his difficulties. The cardinal features are a pronounced impairment of *recent memory*, a tendency to *confabu-*

late, and a disturbed *sense of time*. In other respects the person-ality is well preserved. Of necessity the history should be obtained from an independent informant, as that provided by the patient might well be unreliable.

Impairment of recent memory

While the patient is able to give a reasonably adequate account of himself with regard to his past life and past events, there is a striking impairment of his ability to recall recent events or retain new memories for more than a matter of minutes. The examiner should introduce himself carefully to the patient, asking him to repeat his name at least once to insure that it was clearly under-stood. While continuing to converse with the patient a time interval should be allowed to pass. Generally two to four minutes would be adequate, the patient then being asked to give the examiner's name. He may then deny having been told or evade the question in some other way. When repeated the name might be recognised but again not recalled after a short interval. This test can be repeated by asking the patient to recall an address, or two or three unrelated objects. The inability to acquire the information is often most vividly illustrated by ask-ing the patient to learn the following Babcock sentence — *The one thing a nation needs in order to be rich and great is a large secure supply of wood.* While the patient might well repeat the sentence accurately immediately after hearing it, it is completely forgotten within a matter of minutes. This selective memory impairment applies to all recent events, but there is a striking contrast with the way in which more remote events prior to the onset of the illness will be recalled with reasonable accuracy.

Confabulation

The patient will frequently fill the gaps in his memory with plausible statements. It is only by checking with some indepen-dent source that it will become clear that these statements are inaccurate. The patient will readily reply to questions such as, 'What did you have for breakfast?'; 'How did you spend yesterday?'; 'Who's been to see you lately?' and so on. Unlike a person who is deliberately lying the patient does not seem to appreciate that his reply is in fact inaccurate and will rarely question the correct reply once this is made known to him. It has been suggested that the patient fills the gaps in his recent memory in this way because he is embarrassed by his lack of awareness of such simple information.

Disturbed time sense

Although the patient's orientation in a general sense is usually satisfactory, there is often some disturbance of his ability to estimate time intervals. This might reflect the impairment of recent memory. The following questions might reveal this particular difficulty. 'How long have you been in hospital?'; 'How long would you say we've been talking together?'; 'When were you last examined?'; 'How long ago was your last holiday?' The inaccuracy of replies to such questions are another form of confabulation, but the impairment is much more pronounced than other aspects of orientation.

DEMENTIA

Dementia is a chronic organic syndrome and can be defined as an irreversible decline of cognitive function associated with structural disease of the brain. Most cases of dementia are found amongst elderly people, who often are readily fatigued and have poor concentration, and thus tend to be easily irritated unless approached in a patient, friendly and sympathetic manner. Deafness only adds to the difficulty of assessment.

The diagnosis will usually be clear from a reliable history obtained from some independent source. If dementia is suspected, the examiner should pay special attention to the following aspects of the *history*.

1 Features that would reflect the developing impairment of memory and orientation.

2 Special emphasis on those aspects of the history that could indicate a *cause* of the dementia.

3 Any evidence indicating a *change* in the patient's usual personality.

Developing impairment of memory and orientation

On occasions the patient might complain of having a poor memory, but more commonly this has to be inferred from a change in his behaviour that is likely to be noted by the patient himself as well as those around him. In the early stages of developing dementia it might be recalled that the patient seemed rather more forgetful than usual, at times having difficulty recalling such well known things as his telephone number, address and family birthdays. He might have started to use a notebook to assist his memory, no longer be able to do simple calculations in his head, and to seem to have difficulty in giving or receiving the correct change. As the condition progresses and the severity of the memory impairment increases, the history will reflect this change in a more obvious way. Typical examples will be the patient turning on the gas but forgetting to light it, going out shopping and repeatedly buying the same article, or trying to cook with empty utensils.

Similarly the patient's growing disorientation can be inferred from an independent account of his behaviour. This might reveal such tendencies as going out shopping at night, repeatedly getting lost while out, going to bed during the day, misplacing articles in the home and not knowing where to look for them.

A carefully taken history will thus point to behaviour attributable to impaired memory and orientation, these being cardinal features of dementia.

The cause of the dementia

It would not be appropriate to list all the known causes of dementia, but when taking the history from a patient who is suspected of suffering from that condition, the examiner should always have in mind the more common causes as this will insure that appropriate inquiries are made. A useful framework which can form the basis for such special inquiries are the familiar headings — Congenital, Traumatic, Inflammatory, Neoplastic, Toxic, Metabolic and Degenerative. A few examples will be given, illustrating how each of these headings leads to appropriate inquiries in the history which might help to elucidate the cause of the dementing process.

Congenital or genetic: Is there a family history of Huntington's Chorea?

Traumatic: Has there been a recent head injury? Could the patient's occupation lead to brain damage? eg boxing. Any history of brain surgery?

Inflammatory: Is there a history of venereal disease? Has the patient ever had encephalitis?

Neoplastic: Anything to suggest a primary malignant tumour resulting in cerebral involvement? Are there symptoms suggesting raised intracranial pressure?

Toxic: Is there a history of alcoholism? Has the patient ever attempted suicide by coal gas poisoning?

Metabolic: Any evidence suggesting avitaminosis? Any endocrine disease? eg hypothyroidism, hypoglycaemia.

Degenerative: Any history of stroke or transitory neurological symptoms? Any history of heart disease that could lead to emboli or severe hypotension?

Personality change

The personality of the demented patient frequently changes so that he becomes a caricature of his usual self. His characteristic traits become more pronounced. To establish such a change it will obviously be necessary to have a clear and reliable account of his usual personality as well as a description of the way in which he has altered. Additional features arise from a loss of inhibition and discretion that the patient previously exercised and this can result in antisocial behaviour such as indecent exposure, shoplifiting or similar offences. Neglect of personal hygiene and incontinence are features of the advanced stage of the disease process.

The history of personality change is the most difficult to establish with confidence and also of less diagnostic importance than other aspects of the history.

Mental state

The most prominent features in the *mental state* of the demented patient are impairment of *memory, orientation* and *concentration*. There may be associated *affective* changes and occasional *delusional* beliefs.

Memory impairment and disorientation

Memory can be defined as the voluntary recall of past events and its impairment is perhaps the most prominent feature of dementia. Some consideration has already been given to the assessment of recent memory but in dementia the impairment becomes more generalised or global even though there remains a tendency for more remote memories to be more easily re-called than recent ones. Evidence for memory impairment will have emerged from the history as indicated above. It will also be clear that the patient has difficulty in giving a chronological account of himself, tending to be vague, or evasive about details of his past life or present problems.

Similarly, evidence suggesting that the patient is *disorientated* will have emerged from the history, and its clinical assessment has been discussed in detail above.

In all cases it is advisable to use a simple structured test of memory orientation and concentration. Several standardised schedules are available for this purpose (Blessed *et al* 1968;

Hodkinson 1972; Post 1965). It has been shown, however, that a relatively short series of questions reveals information that is comparable with relatively long and complicated schedules. Furthermore, a short list of questions has the advantage that the examiner can easily commit these to memory and use the same technique in *all* patients, thus providing a better basis for his clinical judgement than when a series of random and variable questions are used.

Two simple standard tests are suggested. These are the '10-Questions Mental Test' (Qureshi & Hodkinson 1974) and the 'Set Test' (Isaacs & Akhtar 1972). The 10 questions are:

1 Age.
2 Time (nearest hour).
3 An address for recall at end of test.
4 Year.
5 Name of institution.
6 Recognition of two persons (doctor/nurse).
7 Date of birth.
8 Years of World War I.
9 Monarch.
10 Count backwards from 20 to 1.

A score of one is given for each question and a total of less than 7 suggests dementia.

In the 'Set Test', the patient is asked to name up to 10 items in each of the following categories:

Animals   Fruit   Colours   Towns

The maximum score is 40. Dementia is the likely diagnosis with a score of less than 15 and unlikely if over 25. More comprehensive clinical tests are available such as the Gresham Ward Questionnaire and the Felix Post Unit Questionnaire (Institute of Psychiatry Maudsley Hospital 1987).

Such tests are never diagnostic in themselves, however, and the results must always be considered in relation to the overall clinical findings. Thus, severe depression can seriously impair a patient's performance on such tests, as can any situation where he is distractible or uncooperative. Nevertheless, increasing familiarity with a simple standard procedure will provide the examiner with the clinical experience on which his assessment of the patient's memory, orientation, and concentration can be based in a meaningful way.

Although impairment of memory, orientation and concentration are central to the diagnosis of dementia, associated features can include *emotional lability* and *delusions*, especially paranoid delusions (see p. 58).

No assessment of the patient, thought to be suffering from an organic syndrome, will be complete unless a careful *physical* examination is also undertaken.

REFERENCES

BICKERSTAFF, E. R. (1980) *Neurological Examination in Clinical Practice*, 4e. Blackwell Scientific Publications, Oxford.

BLESSED, G., TOMLINSON, B. E. & ROTH, M. (1968) The association between quantitative measures of dementia and senile damage in cerebral grey matter of elderly subjects. *British Journal of Psychiatry* **114**, 797–812.

HODKINSON, H. M. (1972) Evaluation of a mental test score for assessment of mental impairment in the elderly. *Age and Ageing* **1**, 233–8.

INSTITUTE OF PSYCHIATRY MAUDSLEY HOSPITAL (1987) *Notes Eliciting and Recording Clinical Information: Psychiatric Examination.* pp. 36–40, 2e. Oxford University Press, Oxford.

ISAACS, B. & AKHTAR, J. (1972) The Set Test: a rapid test of mental function in old people. *Age and Ageing* **1**, 222–6.

MEADOWS, J. C. (1975) The clinical assessment of higher cerebral function. *British Journal of Hospital Medicine* **14**, 273–80.

POST, F. (1965) *The Clinical Psychiatry of Late Life.* pp. 33–4, 47–51. Pergamon Press, Oxford.

QURESHI, K. N. & HODKINSON, H. M. (1974) Evaluation of a 10-Question Test in the institutionalised elderly. *Age and Ageing* **3**, 152–7.

Difficult Patients

The scheme of history-taking and eliciting signs and symptoms presented so far is ideal, in that it presupposes adequate understanding of the questions by the patient and reasonably precise answers. This is by no means always the case. In this chapter, various problems that interfere with communication between interviewer and patient will be discussed and means of tackling them will be presented.

LANGUAGE PROBLEMS

Patients who speak little or no English not uncommonly present to the psychiatrist practising in a city. They are either recent immigrants or else foreign born women who have been here some time but have been sheltered from contact with English people. It is imperative to obtain an interpreter. Usually a member of the family who can speak English volunteers for the job, but this is unsatisfactory for a variety of reasons. Firstly, the relative may not be familiar with the relevant psychiatric terms and secondly, he may be reluctant to divulge information that could present the family in an unfavourable light. For these reasons psychiatric departments should maintain lists of interpreters who are willing to act for members of the local immigrant communities. However, even an interpreter is not foolproof. Mostly they are reluctant to reveal any gaps in their knowledge of English and in preference will use an inappropriate word. The interviewer should therefore take particular care with non-verbal observations of the patient (see Chapter Four).

Deaf mute patients, although much rarer, present the same

problems. An interpreter who knows sign language should be used if the patient is conversant with this.

Among English speaking people there is considerable variation in the degree to which emotional distress is expressed cognitively. In general, patients with poorer education and less medical sophistication tend to express themselves more in somatic than in cognitive terms. Thus, instead of complaining of depression or anxiety, they focus on palpitations, peculiar feelings in the head, or tension in the stomach. This may delay recognition of a psychiatric complaint and lead to unnecessary investigations for physical illness. A careful history will often reveal the correct diagnosis. Patients who present a variety of somatic symptoms should be asked if there is any diurnal variation. An account of somatic symptoms that are worse first thing in the morning and improve during the day is good evidence of a depressive illness. Impaired concentration and poor sleep and appetite may also be present in the absence of depressed mood, and add support to the diagnosis.

Anxiety that is presented entirely somatically is more difficult to diagnose, but an account of episodic symptoms should alert the interviewer to this possibility, particularly if excessive sweating is a predominant feature. Of course, hyperthyroidism has to be considered in the differential diagnosis. Depersonalisation and derealisation should be inquired about, as symptoms associated with anxiety. The patient should also be asked if the somatic symptoms occur in any particular situations, as phobic anxiety may present in a purely somatic form. Faintness or giddiness occurring only when the patient is out-of-doors, or only when he is alone, indicates a phobia.

PROBLEMS DUE TO PSYCHOTIC SYMPTOMS

Mutism and stupor

Patients suffering from severe psychomotor retardation take a long time to answer questions, may fail to answer some questions altogether, and often give monosyllabic replies. This makes interviewing very difficult and the examiner should restrict himself to a few key questions aimed at eliciting the prevailing affect and the first rank symptoms of schizophrenia. Severe retardation may progress to mutism, or the patient may present in the first instance with complete absence of speech. In either case it is essential to obtain as full a history as possible from informants. Although little can be gained by asking the patient questions, some clues as to the diagnosis may be picked up from his non-verbal behaviour.

In hysterical mutism, the patient is not physically retarded and will often communicate with the interviewer in writing. He may even be persuaded to whisper or to mouth words. Mutism may be accompanied by complete physical inactivity, in which case the patient's state is called stupor. The level of consciousness may be lowered, but is difficult to assess under such conditions. The mute patient who is not completely inactive may exhibit mannerisms or posturing (see p. 32), indicating a diagnosis of schizophrenia. A full neurological examination should be carried out on every stuporose patient to rule out organic brain disease. The examiner should note whether the patient's eyes are open or shut, and if open whether they are set in a fixed stare, roam about the room aimlessly, or follow people about. He should give the patient various commands, such as 'open your eyes' or 'lift your left arm', and note whether they are obeyed. The tone of the limbs should be tested, and the limbs placed in awkward positions, to see if the patient will hold them there. If the tone is uniformly increased and the patient maintains uncomfortable postures for minutes at a time, waxy flexibility is present and the diagnosis is catatonia. Patients with catatonia may also show resistiveness; active resistance to attempts to move them. Excessive greasiness of the skin is another indicator of catatonia.

The prevailing affect may be assessed by examination of the patient's facial expression. In catatonic stupor the expression is completely blank, whereas in depressive stupor the patient often maintains a fixed expression of misery (see p. 34).

Diagnosis of the psychiatric condition producing stupor is often difficult until the stupor resolves. The patient should then be questioned carefully about his experiences while stuporose. However, if the stupor has been terminated by electroconvulsive therapy, the patient is unlikely to remember very much and the diagnosis may remain in doubt.

Speech disorder

The patient's speech may be so disturbed that the examiner is unable to obtain relevant answers to any of his questions. The form of the speech disorder should be carefully noted, using the transcript of an audio-recording if necessary, and may be sufficient to suggest a diagnosis (see p. 42). If not, then the interviewer should pay particular attention to the patient's non-verbal behaviour. Rapid speech which makes it difficult for the interviewer to get a word in edgeways, physical overactivity, and a euphoric mood are indicative of mania. Speech of normal speed and blunted affect suggest schizophrenia. It is always worth re-assessing the patient when the speech disorder has resolved, either spontaneously or with treatment, as additional pathology may then be elicited to substantiate a diagnosis.

Overactivity

Physical overactivity may be so extreme as to prevent a full interview being conducted. Patients who are unable to sit still for more than a few minutes and who have to get up and pace about the room may be suffering from agitated depression, mania, or catatonic excitement. The examiner should restrict himself to a few key questions and concentrate on the patient's non-verbal behaviour. The assessment of affect is clearly crucial for the differential diagnosis. The patient should be reinterviewed once the overactivity has been controlled.

Distractibility

This is a feature of mania (see p. 39) and often prevents the patient from attending to the interviewer's questions. Therefore, the initial interview should be kept as short as possible, with a concentration on the patient's affect and non-verbal behaviour. It will be necessary to reassess the patient when this symptom subsides.

PROBLEMS DUE TO NEUROTIC SYMPTOMS

Impaired concentration

A number of neurotic conditions, including depression and anxiety, can severely impair the patient's concentration. This makes it difficult for the patient to take in everything the interviewer asks him. He may also lose the thread of his answer, and forget what the question was, before he has completed it. The interviewer must be prepared to take his time with such patients, to wait while they collect their thoughts, repeat questions if the patient forgets them, and prompt them gently for their answers.

Obsessions

Obsessional patients sometimes find it hard to bring their answers to a conclusion because of doubts, hesitations and modifications. Thus, they may give an initially positive answer to a question, but then introduce so many qualifications that it is virtually transformed into a negative. This is both confusing for the interviewer and time-consuming. In contrast to all previous advice on interviewing patients, the psychiatrist should deal with such obsessional responses by cutting across the patient after his initial response and steering him on to the next question. This needs to be done politely but firmly.

PROBLEMS DUE TO ORGANIC CONDITIONS

The restless, perplexed, bewildered and frightened, delirious patient can be difficult to examine and it is especially necessary for the examiner to clearly identify himself to the patient. When possible it is helpful if a relative or friend is present to reassure the patient and if necessary to remind him of the purpose of the examination. The examination should be carried out in a well-lit room and sometimes the patient can most easily be interviewed in the context of a more familiar 'medical' approach by the examiner, such as by taking his blood pressure, feeling the pulse, examining the tongue or taking the temperature. This is particularly appropriate in the assessment of a delirious patient, although a more comprehensive physical examination may not be possible until the restlessness and overactivity have been brought under control. When the delirium is clearly due to alcohol withdrawal (delirium tremens) and appropriate facilities are not immediately available, the patient can be made more approachable by giving him an alcoholic drink as an emergency measure.

Problems of communication are often experienced with organic patients, especially if elderly. Unless a patient's deafness can be overcome the assessment will be inconclusive. The examiner should always be prepared to address the patient in a loud voice, speaking in a slow deliberate manner with carefully enunciated words giving the patient an opportunity to lip read if possible. Use of a hearing-aid or ear-trumpet can be helpful, but on occasions one may have to resort to laborious writing in order to communicate with the patient. Similarly, a blind patient must be approached in a tactful way to allay fear and anxiety. Again the presence of a person who is familiar to the patient will be helpful, and the patient may become more relaxed and reassured if the examiner maintains some physical contact with the patient such as by holding his hand or arm during the examination.

Patients suffering from organic disorders are especially liable to become fatigued and lose concentration if the examination is prolonged. They might even become irritable, antagonistic and uncooperative, and in such circumstances it is clearly unwise to persevere with the examination. Allow the patient to rest and resume the examination after a reasonable interval.

PROBLEMS DUE TO PATIENTS' ATTITUDES

Suspicion

Suspicious patients may be wary of the whole interviewing procedure, may want to know the purpose of the questions, and may wish for confirmation of the interviewer's authority to ask them. They should be reassured on all these matters. It is advisable never to smile at paranoid patients or to try to joke with them. These attempts to produce a relaxed atmosphere will often be misinterpreted by the patient as maliciously directed at him.

Hostility

The hostile or aggressive patient should be handled cautiously. If the interviewer has any reason to anticipate violence he should make sure that other staff are within calling distance. It is also advisable for the interviewer to sit nearer the door than the patient and to have a desk between himself and the patient. Patients who become impatient and irritable with the interviewing procedure can rarely be persuaded to sit through the rest of the interview. It is preferable to break off at that point and return to complete the interview later.

Denial

Some patients answer every question in the negative, but leave the examiner with the impression that they are concealing a lot of pathology. In this case a note to that effect should be recorded and particular attention paid to obtaining full accounts of the history from informants.

Compliance

Other patients say 'yes' to every question, so that the interviewer does not know what to credit and what to disbelieve. It is with these patients that the crossquestioning approach is particularly important (see p. 49). With these compliant patients, a symptom should be judged as present only if the patient gives a detailed account of the necessary experience in his own words.

Malingering

If the interviewer suspects that the patient is feigning illness, he should ask simple factual questions such as 'What colour is grass?' If the answer given is 'blue' or some other response that indicates that the patient knows the correct answer and is deliberately distorting it, then he is almost certainly malingering. In this case the rest of the interview should be discounted.

Psychiatric Examination
of Children

The principles of taking a history and examining the patient are the same for children as for adults, however, there are some important differences between the two situations. Children rarely, if ever, have an awareness of being ill in a psychiatric sense or of needing the services of a psychiatrist, although they may be conscious of having a problem. Therefore they cannot formulate complaints in the way an adult patient usually can. Instead the interviewer has to rely on the parents to present what they view as the child's complaints, and often on other people as well, such as the general practitioner or the school-teacher.

Children referred to the psychiatrist range in age from the toddler stage to adolescence. This range encompasses vast differences in motor and verbal abilities and in social competence, so that the interviewer must be prepared to adapt his techniques of assessment to suit the level reached by the individual child. Many of the children brought to a psychiatrist are too young to be interviewed in the manner customary with adult patients. They cannot be sat in a chair and asked questions. Instead the interviewer will have to provide a more 'natural' and informal situation in which the child's interest can be engaged. Playing with toys and materials is a natural and familiar activity for younger children. The interviewer needs to provide a set-up which allows him to watch the child at play and also enables him to interact with the child so as to observe his social behaviour. Once the child has been put at ease in this manner, he may give informative responses to more direct questioning.

REFERRAL

Because children never refer themselves to a psychiatrist, although the occasional adolescent may do so, it is important for the interviewer to appreciate the reasons behind the referral. Sometimes a normal child is referred by parents because they have made him a scapegoat for their own problems. Occasionally parents will refer a child with relatively minor symptoms instead of his sibling who is much more disturbed. A general practitioner may refer a child whose parents need treatment but are resistant to it, in the hope that the referral will involve them in some therapy. Sometimes, a string of referrals will come from a particular schoolteacher who may be intolerant of minor behavioural problems, which most teachers could cope with quite adequately. These examples make it clear that the process of referral has to be carefully considered in the context of the child's family setting and the wider social setting, in addition to focusing on the actual complaints.

HISTORY-TAKING

In most cases the child will be accompanied by his mother and father, from whom the history will be taken. If the father does not appear on the first visit, he should be encouraged to come subsequently as he is often as important as the mother in the genesis of the child's symptoms. In the case of an adolescent, the patient should be interviewed first on his own, followed by the parents. With younger children, the interviewer usually has a choice of seeing the child separately from his parents or interviewing the family together. Both have their advantages and disadvantages. Children seen together with their parents are rarely open about their problems. On the other hand the joint interview is the best way of observing how the family actually functions. If the parents are to be seen separately from the child, someone usually has to be available to look after the child. Some children of preschool age refuse to be separated from their parents. If the child strongly resists separation, it is wrong for the interviewer to force the issue and leave a screaming child for a staff member to cope with. Separate interviews and family interviews have been presented here as alternatives, but in any ongoing treatment situation the interviewer will gain valuable information from using each technique to supplement the other.

When obtaining a history from the parents it must be remembered that their accounts are inevitably coloured by their emotional attitudes towards the child. For example, a parent who feels guilty about possibly contributing to the child's condition is likely to cover up what may be seen as abnormalities, and to present as normal an account as possible. The parent's emotional attitudes concerning the child are an important part of the situation, so that while taking the history the interviewer should both assess these attitudes and attempt to evaluate their effect on the account he obtains. Furthermore, he should endeavour to obtain information from other sources whenever possible. It must be emphasised that a child's disturbed behaviour may be restricted to particular situations. He can show severe disturbance at home, but act perfectly normally at school, or vice versa.

In general, information about the child's early years is much less reliable than data concerning the present. Therefore, while the interviewer must not neglect the patient's early childhood, he should concentrate more on the child's current behaviour. When dealing with this he should not be content with general comments from his informants such as 'he is difficult at bedtime', but must press for detailed descriptions of actual behaviour and situations. As with adult patients, it is extremely valuable to ask for an account of a typical day (see p. 10).

Any difficulties elicited should be related in time to the child's general development and particular events, such as parental absences, birth of siblings, or change of school. The interviewer should attempt to determine whether anything made the difficulty better or worse, including any treatment that may have been given. He should also inquire about the course of each difficulty, in particular whether it is improving or deteriorating.

Difficulties shown by children are often quantitatively rather than qualitatively abnormal. This poses to the interviewer the problem of deciding how severe a disturbance in behaviour has to be before it can be considered a symptom. In making this decision, it is helpful to be guided by the extent of suffering caused by the disturbance either in the child or in others around him.

PRESENT COMPLAINTS

The parents' complaints about the child may largely reflect their own psychopathology, or difficulties in their marital relationship. A vital part of the assessment of the child is therefore an impression of the parents' mental health and the quality of their marriage. The interviewer must have this in the forefront of his mind when seeing the parents, and should take note of their reported response to the child's behaviour.

Complaints are unlikely to be presented in an orderly or consistent fashion, either by parents or by other informants, such as schoolteachers. Nevertheless, the interviewer should allow the initial account to be as spontaneous as possible, since it will at least reflect the informant's main concerns. Apart from this, it is a distinct advantage for the interviewer to have an organised scheme in mind, in order to explore all possible areas of the child's functioning, even if they are not referred to spontaneously. The following scheme is set out as one way of organising an inquiry into present complaints.

Emotional disturbances

Complaints in this area, when presented about the adolescent or older child, are virtually identical to neurotic symptoms in adults (see Chapter Seven). They include depression, suicidal ideas or attempts, general anxiety, separation anxiety, phobias, including school refusal, hypochondriasis, obsessions, hysterical symptoms, and excessive irritability, including temper tantrums.

Reliance on the parents' account is likely to lead to underdiagnosis of emotional disturbances, in that they are often unaware of quite marked misery in their children. In taking a history, the age of the child must be borne in mind as frequent crying, whining, nightmares and poor appetite occur less often in older children than in younger.

Disturbance in relationships

The norms that are applied to the way children get on with members of their social circle vary considerably from social class to social class, and from subculture to subculture. Furthermore, there is also considerable variation between families belonging to the same social group, depending on the personalities and levels of tolerance of the individuals concerned. Due allowance must be made for this in evaluating complaints about disturbance in the child's relationships. The relationships that need to be inquired about are those within the nuclear family (parents and siblings), or the extended family if appropriate (grandparents, uncles and aunts), those with adults outside the family, particularly at school, and those with peers (friends and classmates). Parents are unreliable in reporting about the child's relationships with siblings and peers, so that more credence should be given to accounts of these from schoolteachers and from the child himself. Children have been shown to be reliable in their reporting of their peer relationships. In assessing relationships, the interviewer should ask about the giving and receiving of affection, including how demonstrative the child is, the response to authority figures in terms of compliance or non-compliance, and the amount of communication that occurs.

Physical symptoms

Sleeping and eating disorders in children are commonly the manifestation of emotional tension, although sleep disturbance only emerges in relation to depression in later adolescence. Inquiry should be made about disturbance of sleep patterns, nightmares, walking or talking during sleep, refusal to eat, excessive food fads (most children have *some* food fads), pica (the ingestion of inedible material such as paint), delay in establishing urinary or faecal continence, or loss of continence after it has been established. Questions should be asked about headaches, bodily pains, nausea and fainting, as these may also represent manifestations of emotional tension. The child's general health should be inquired into as there is an association between physical illness and emotional disturbance.

Behavioural disturbance

Motor behaviour
Both increased and reduced motor activity may be abnormal if present in severe degree. Many parents complain that their child is overactive, but the important question is the appropriateness of this behaviour. The interviewer needs to determine the setting of the overactivity in order to assess its inappropriateness. Movements may also be abnormal in quality, as with clumsiness or poor coordination. Repetitive movements should be inquired about and include tics, twiddling of fingers, twirling of the body, rocking and head banging.

The child's ability to concentrate should be assessed by asking how easily he is distracted from leisure activities such as reading or games, or from carrying out tasks.

Verbal behaviour

The development of speech or comprehension may be delayed, the articulation of words may be disordered, or there may be disturbances of speech rhythm, as in stammering. The quality of speech may be abnormal, as in childhood autism, or speech after developing normally may disappear, as in elective mutism.

Antisocial behaviour

Antisocial behaviour may be directed against the parents, other authority figures, or the child's peers. Behaviour such as disobedience, lying, stealing, destructiveness to objects, aggressiveness to people, arson, and truancy may be complained of by parents or schoolteachers, and should be inquired about if not mentioned spontaneously. It should be borne in mind, however, that parents are particularly unreliable in assessing disobedience.

Family history

This can be covered in exactly the same way as with an adult patient (see Chapter Three). An additional bonus when the patient is a child is that the interviewer is able to form a direct impression of at least one of the parents.

History of patient's childhood

This should start with the mother's pregnancy. Firstly the interviewer should determine whether the pregnancy was planned or accidental, and if the latter, the parents' attitudes to the continuation of the pregnancy.

Any complications of pregnancy should be noted, also any severe infection during pregnancy, particularly German measles. Details of the birth should be inquired about and any abnormality recorded. The mother should also be asked about the condition of the child at birth, although she may not be able to supply reliable information. All these details are important as they may suggest causes of early brain damage.

The duration of breast feeding should be determined and the child's reaction to weaning. The milestones of development need to be recorded. Parents' memory of these is not as accurate as might be expected, and if a written record was made at the time either by the parents or by a professional person, eg in a Well Baby Clinic, this should be obtained. The interviewer should endeavour to determine the age of first smiling, holding up the head, sitting up, crawling, walking, first words and first sentences, continence of urine and faeces by night and day, and ability to dress unaided. The interviewer must have a good idea of the age range of achievement of these milestones in the normal population.

Any signs of emotional disturbance in early childhood should be ascertained. The parent should be asked about nightmares, sleepwalking, other sleep difficulties, fear of the dark, fears of animals or of specific situations, temper tantrums, and loss of control of urine or faeces once this has been established.

Separations from either parent during childhood should be inquired about, and the child's reaction to these ascertained. The reason for the separation should be determined, as the child's response to death of a parent is likely to be quite different from his reaction to the break-up of his parents' marriage. The interviewer should also ask about his response to the birth of younger siblings if there are any.

Schooling

If the child is of school age, or has attended a preschool playgroup or day-nursery, the interviewer should ask about his reaction to being left with other adults in these situations. The child's ability to learn in the classroom needs to be determined, bearing in mind the possibility of a specific reading disorder in a child of otherwise normal intelligence. Inquiry also needs to be made about the relationships he has developed with teachers and with other children. Particularly in the younger child the nature of play activities is as important as academic achievement. The balance of fantasy and reality both in his play and in his written productions should be ascertained. A complete lack of fantasy is as abnormal as a total preoccupation with fantasy, and may indicate mental subnormality or severe emotional inhibition. These aspects of the child's behaviour at school are unlikely to be known to the parents in any detail. Therefore it is desirable, if not essential, to obtain a report about the child from his form teacher or the headmaster of the school. If the child has been seen by a school medical officer, his opinion should also be requested. The results of psychological tests that may have been carried out on the child as part of the school's assessment procedures should be obtained.

Previous illnesses

A history of serious illnesses, hospital admissions, and operations needs to be taken. If thought to be relevant, the notes of any hospital admissions should be requested.

Sexual development

Masturbation often starts from the earliest years and is quite normal unless it occupies a considerable proportion of the child's waking hours. In assessing this, allowance must be made for parents' embarrassed or repressive attitudes which can colour their account of their child's masturbation.

If the patient is pubertal, an account of the development of interest in the opposite sex should be obtained. The onset of periods in girls and of the voice breaking and the need to shave in boys should be dated. This is also an appropriate point to introduce questions about crossdressing in childhood. Adult transvestites almost always give a history of crossdressing during their early years.

Temperamental characteristics

Although personality, as distinct from symptoms, is given some weight in adult patients it receives little attention in children. It is commonly believed that the personality is relatively unformed until adulthood. Nevertheless, many mothers recognise striking differences in temperament between their children from birth onwards. Certain temperamental characteristics have been shown to be linked with disturbed behaviour in children and should be inquired about. They are as follows:

Intensity of mood
This is assessed from the way the child shows his feelings, both positive and negative, in a variety of situations. The informant should be asked how the child expresses his feelings in specific situations such as being amused or being upset by something. Accounts of the child habitually roaring with laughter, screaming with rage, or bawling his eyes out must be taken special note of.

Negative mood
Inquiry about the child's expression of feelings also provides an opportunity to assess the balance between a positive mood, such as cheerfulness and pleasure, and a negative mood, such as sadness, anger and tension. The child who shows a persistently negative mood is at risk for behavioural or emotional disorder.

Malleability
The informant should be asked how easy or difficult it is to persuade the child to do something else when he is engaged on a particular activity. Children who stick rigidly to what they are doing, despite determined attempts to alter their behaviour, are more vulnerable to behavioural or emotional disorder.

Regularity
Disturbed children also exhibit less regularity in their biological functioning. To ascertain the presence of irregularity, the interviewer needs to ask about the child's patterns of sleeping and waking, eating at meal times and between meals, and his bowel habits.

Fastidiousness

Tolerance of mess is another temperamental characteristic linked with behavioural or emotional disorder. The interviewer should inquire about the child's reaction to making a mess at mealtimes or at play, to getting his clothes dirty or to wetting or soiling his underthings, and in any other similar situation.

Social circumstances

To round off the history it is essential to obtain an account of the family's social circumstances. In particular it is important to know how many rooms they inhabit and whether the child shares a room or a bed with any other family member. The financial position of the family should be inquired about as this can influence the way the child is treated, for example his nutrition, the number of playthings available, whether he wears new clothes or cast-offs, and the possibility of day-nursery placement.

PRESENT MENTAL STATE

Preliminary observations

The observation of the child starts in the waiting room. The interviewer has an opportunity to begin to assess the parent–child relationship, and any gross physical abnormalities in the child before the interview begins. Clues as to the nature of the parent–child relationship may be found in the way the child is dressed, the way he behaves while waiting to be seen, and his reaction to being separated from his parent.

Physical abnormalities

Certain unusual features of the face or of body build can suggest a likely diagnosis. *Cretinism*, which is typically associated with mental retardation, also produces dwarfism and a characteristic facies with an enlarged and protruding tongue, coarse hair, and a yellowish scaly skin. The child's voice is hoarse. A thyroid swelling is not necessarily present. *Down's syndrome*, in which the IQ ranges from severe retardation to borderline subnormal, also produces a characteristic facies with small slanting palpebral fissures and marked epicanthic folds. The face is flat, the hair coarse and scanty, the nose short with a depressed bridge, the tongue large and fissured, the lower jaw rounded, and the ears small and rounded with a simple pattern of folds. A small number of much rarer conditions also give rise to mental retardation and produce characteristic physical abnormalities. They include *gargoylism*, which distorts the face grotesquely, *tuberosclerosis*, which gives rise to a butterfly-shaped rash on the nose and cheeks. and *Tay–Sachs* disease, in which blindness occurs by the second year.

The body build may be *unusually thin*, in which case the interviewer should suspect *anorexia nervosa*, particularly in pubertal girls. Alternatively the child may be *excessively fat*. This can also occur as a phase in anorexia nervosa, or may be a manifestation of overfeeding by the parents or compulsive eating by the child. In either case the child is likely to be the object of teasing by his peers and to suffer from social ostracism.

Dress

The child may be dressed inappropriately for age or sex. The parents may be responsible for dressing the child in a fashion appropriate either for a much older or a much younger child, reflecting the desire for premature independence or else an attempt to baby their offspring. Clothes may also emphasise femininity in a male child or vice versa, indicating parental dissatisfaction with the sex of their child.

Behaviour

Gross disturbances of behaviour while waiting to be interviewed may be shown by children with mental retardation or childhood autism, and antisocial children. *Mentally retarded* children may show spitting or dribbling, self-injury, such as biting their knuckles or arms, and repetitive movements such as rocking or head banging. *Autistic* children may also show these features, but in addition are likely to exhibit flicking of their fingers in front of their eyes, jumping up and down and flapping their arms, spinning round, a peculiar gait, such as walking on tiptoe, and intense piercing screaming. Their social behaviour is also likely to be peculiar: they show no awareness of the presence of other people in the waiting room and no social response to the interviewer when he approaches them. *Antisocial* children may be very aggressive while waiting, either to their parents, to other people in the room, or to inanimate objects. The attitude of their parents to this behaviour should be taken note of, in particular any attempts to control it and whether they are effective. While this kind of behaviour may be shown by younger children, older children are often able to control their antisocial behaviour and to present an impression of complete normality to the interviewer.

As mentioned earlier, preschool children may resist attempts to separate them from either parent. The child's reaction to this situation depends on age, on previous experience of separations, and on parental attitudes to letting the child go. The need to interview the child alone provides a good opportunity to assess the latter. As already emphasised, the interviewer should not insist on removing the child from his parents if he becomes very distressed by it.

THE INTERVIEW

The interview has different functions according to the age of the child. An adolescent can be asked questions formally as with an adult patient and is usually able to give a good account of any neurotic symptoms he suffers from, including depression. Even children of 7 or 8 are capable of describing pathological guilt or hopelessness convincingly. A younger child is unlikely to give useful responses to formal questions, but may make informative spontaneous remarks while playing. Even under these circumstances a direct expression of depression is rare and has to be inferred from the content of the child's play and from non-verbal communication. However, fears and anxieties are often voiced directly by the younger child.

Because of the varied needs of children at different ages, the interview room needs to be furnished so that the interaction with the child can be on a formal level of dialogue or an informal level of play. Thus there has to be a desk with two or more chairs as well as play facilities. It is advisable for the interviewer to have a limited range of toys with which he is familiar, so that he has a reasonable idea of what uses children of different ages are likely to make of them. They should include a number of objects that can be used for performance tasks, such as building-bricks and jigsaws, dolls and miniature accessories for imaginative play, and drawing materials for constructive activity. A selection of psychological tests is also necessary; the nature of these will be discussed below. It will make the room less intimidating to children if there are bright pictures or posters on the walls, or possibly the paintings and drawings of other children.

The interview has a different value relative to the history according to the kind of disturbance the child exhibits. For instance it has little to contribute to the evaluation of disturbed peer relationships, which are best assessed from the history. On the other hand, it is crucial for the direct observation of the symptoms of autism and hyperkinesis.

Many children, including those who are quite normal, show nervousness on entering the interview room for the first time, so the interviewer need not pay much attention to this, except to try to put the child at ease. The child's non-verbal behaviour should then be observed for any abnormalities.

Non-verbal behaviour

Motor activity

This may be excessive or reduced in quantity, or abnormal in quality. Hyperactivity is seen in children as a manifestation of *brain dysfunction, mental retardation, emotional disturbance*, or any combination of these. It will almost certainly be evident while the child is in the waiting room, as such children find it very difficult to sit still for long, but move about ceaselessly. The constant activity interrupts any task they attempt to settle down to, so that there is an aimless quality to their restlessness. A child with marked hypermotility is impossible to interview in a formal way unless under sedation. The overactivity is usually associated with impulsiveness as well as short attention span.

Some children move about much less than normal. The interviewer should take note of the child who shows no interest in exploring the interview room and the toys and play materials provided. Such children may sit in a chair with very little movement at all throughout the interview. This immobility can be due to *severe mental retardation*, to *depression or anxiety*, or simply to *shyness*.

Motor behaviour may be qualitatively abnormal in a variety of ways. Children may show *incoordination* of movements, which in a mild form presents as occasional clumsiness. If this is only seen in particular situations, where the child is likely to feel self-conscious, it is almost certainly emotional in origin. Persistent incoordination may occur as an isolated symptom, when it is likely to represent a developmental anomaly. In some cases, however, there is associated brain damage. *Stereotypies*, or repetitive movements, and *fidgeting* are seen commonly among normal children, as well as in antisocial children so need not be taken special note of, unless they have a bizarre character, as in *childhood autism*. Children with this condition repeatedly flick their fingers in front of their eyes, jump up and down flapping their hands, rock backwards and forwards from one foot to

127

another, twirl round and round, and perform other gross repetitive movements.

Relationship with interviewer

The relationship the child develops with the interviewer provides important clues as to diagnosis. The interviewer should observe the child's eye contact with him, how well the child responds in general, and how much he smiles in particular. Reduced eye contact is shown by *autistic children*, and *depressed* children. Autistic children show an active avoidance of gaze and avert their eyes when the examiner looks directly at them. A careful observer may note that the autistic child make rapid flicking movements of his eyes with which he looks directly, but only for an instant at the interviewer. Depressed children may stare in one direction fixedly without looking at the interviewer or their surroundings. Their gaze is often directed downwards.

The child's general response to the interviewer should be appraised, taking note of his liveliness, how much he initiates social interchange and how much he waits for the interviewer to take the lead. *Depressed* children show a very passive attitude to the interview situation. *Anti-social* children may show sullen resistance to the interviewer's overtures or alternatively may be disinhibited or challenging, taking an inappropriately dominant or overfamiliar role. Mentally retarded children may exhibit little social responsiveness, while *autistic* children may treat the interviewer as an object rather than a person, failing to give him any human recognition.

Smiling is the first social response a child develops, and its absence must be taken seriously. It is, of course, a response to the interviewer's own expressed warmth and friendliness, which vary from person-to-person. However, each interviewer has his own interview style and as long as it is consistent he should be able to reliably identify the child who smiles less than usual. Both *neurotic* and *antisocial* children show this abnormality.

Non-verbal expression of affect

The child's expression of emotion is usually more open and less camouflaged than that of an adult. However, inhibited children often keep a tight rein on their emotions and during the interview may betray little of their feelings non-verbally, except for their tense state. This may give a false impression of a less severe disturbance than is actually present.

The main affects to be observed in children are anxiety, depression, anger, and apathy. *Anxiety* is shown by elevation of the eyebrows, which produces horizontal furrows right across the forehead. The eyes are open more widely than normal and the pupils are dilated. *Depression* is shown by overt crying and sobbing, and in the absence of tears by a characteristic facial expression and bodily posture. The eyebrows are drawn upwards at the medial end only, producing a puckering in the centre of the forehead. The palpebral fissures are narrowed, and the corners of the mouth are drawn downwards. The child's gaze is directed at the floor and the head is hunched into the shoulders, which are drawn forward. It is noteworthy that depression is as common among children showing antisocial behaviour as among those with neurotic problems. *Anger* is shown as much in the child's activities as in his facial expression. He may bare his teeth, clench his fists, stamp his feet, or lie on the floor, screaming and kicking in a *temper tantrum*. His destructiveness may be directed at the toys and play materials, the furniture, or even the interviewer himself. It goes almost without saying that the interviewer should curb the child's anger if it reaches this intensity.

Verbal behaviour

The development of speech in a normal fashion is dependent both on the intactness of the brain and the child's emotional state. Delay in acquisition of speech may be due to impairments in either or both spheres. If speech fails to develop at all, the child may be suffering from *deafness*, a *developmental language*

129

disorder, severe mental retardation or *autism*. Many autistic children eventually develop speech, but it is of a peculiar kind. They do not seem able to use language in a symbolic way: words become associated with particular objects instead of representing a class of objects. For example, the word 'ball' may be used for one particular ball of a certain size and colour, instead of for any ball regardless of its size and colour. This inability to generalise also gives rise to difficulties in using pronouns like 'you' and 'me' appropriately.

Where speech development has been normal, the quantity spoken can be affected by functional disorders. Children who are very *shy* or *inhibited* make very few spontaneous remarks, although they may be coaxed by the interviewer into answering some questions. On the other hand, *antisocial* children, who are particularly uninhibited, produce more spontaneous remarks than normal children, and so do *neurotic* children who talk a lot about their problems.

The content of speech, particularly in the older child and adolescent, is of great importance in helping the interviewer come to a diagnosis. In this respect, the remarks the child makes spontaneously are of much greater significance than his answers to the interviewer's questions. Children who make few spontaneous comments in the formal interview situation may be much more forthcoming when playing with toys and materials. The interviewer should be alert for a preoccupation with topics of an anxious or depressive nature. The child may voice fears concerning real objects, animals, people or situations, including fears of change and separation. Alternatively, the fears may relate to imaginary beings such as ghosts and monsters. The child may be concerned with depressive topics such as illness or death. It is very rare for prepubertal children to express suicidal ideas.

Play

The necessity for play materials in the interview situation has already been emphasised. Not only do they help the child feel at ease, but they act as a stimulus to his fantasies and hence encourage spontaneous speech. The way the child uses the play materials and toys also provides clues to the diagnosis. *Autistic* children are unable to indulge in symbolic play; for instance they treat dolls as objects instead of representations of people. *Mentally retarded* children show some ability to use toys symbolically, but it is more or less limited by the degree of retardation.

The child's fantasies developed while playing, focus on his relationships with the people who mean most to him, even though this may not be immediately apparent from the content of the fantasies. For example, games involving kings and queens express something of the child's feelings about his parents. It is not within the scope of this book to discuss the dynamics of the child's relationships which are revealed in this fashion. Nevertheless, a sensitivity on the part of the interviewer to the latent content of the child's fantasies will enable him to detect themes which are expressive of anxiety, depression or aggression, and hence lead him to a diagnosis.

Assessing the child referred for suspected sexual abuse

The increasing awareness of this problem among professionals and the general public makes it incumbent on the psychiatrist to be prepared to carry out an appropriate assessment. The question as to whether or not abuse has occurred will mainly be the responsibility of the police and social workers. However, the psychiatrist faced with a child showing disturbed behaviour may sometimes have to discover whether abuse has occurred in order to understand its origins. Usually, child psychiatrists will not be requested to interview a well child to determine whether sexual abuse has occurred. Exceptionally, however, they may be asked to see children under 5 years, those with learning difficulties, and children involved in divorce and custody disputes.

As with a child referred for any psychiatric condition, it is essential that evaluation should be set in the context of the family. It is necessary to assess the child's relationship with each parent, and the parents' relationships with one another and with significant others. Therefore the child needs to be interviewed in the company of the parents as well as alone. An interview usually provides more reliable evidence than physical examination of the child.

The referred child may be at any developmental stage from the preverbal to adolescence, and the interviewer must be prepared to adapt his approach accordingly. Additionally, children's behaviour and experience, particularly in the sexual realm, vary considerably with culture. The interviewer should be aware of the range of behaviour that is culturally accepted and practised.

Doubts have been expressed about the ability of children to give an accurate account of their past experience. In general, children's memory for events is reasonably accurate, although distortions can be induced by persistent leading questions, and these should obviously be avoided. In attempting to distinguish between a child's fantasies and factual events, it is helpful to bear in mind that the latter are more likely to include detail and sensory information. It is therefore useful to enquire about perceptual experiences, including taste, smell and touch. Additionally the child can be asked hypothetical questions, such as: 'Is this real or pretend?'

The interview should be paced by the child and not by external pressures. It should begin with the establishment of rapport by asking questions about friends, school, pets and hobbies. Later on, questions should be directed at the methods of maintaining discipline in the home, sleeping arrangements, bathing arrangements, and the availability of privacy. The responses may give leads to further questioning. It should be made clear to the child from the beginning, with whom any information will be shared. It is misleading to promise confidentiality if this cannot be guaranteed.

It is important to obtain from the child his personal terms for sexuality and sexual organs and to use these in all discussions. This process can begin with non-sexual body parts and proceed to genitalia. Precocious knowledge of sexual matters beyond what is expected for the child's age group should raise the suspicion of sexual abuse. Such knowledge may be revealed in the detail of drawings of men and women by the child.

Communication can be aided by non-leading, facilitating questions, by the use of toys and materials, and by the creation of an atmosphere of acceptance and safety. Children often reveal only a portion of their experience at first to test the listener's response. If this is non-threatening and supportive, they are likely to supply more details. In this respect, it is essential for the interviewer to contain his emotional response to what may be disturbing and distressing material. Sexually abused children are particularly sensitive to the emotional responses of others.

General facilitating questions, such as: 'Is there anything you feel unhappy about that you'd like to tell me?' can be followed by the more specific: 'Has anyone touched or tickled you in a scary way, or in a private place?' Young children may not be able to verbalize but can draw revealing pictures. The child may be asked to draw himself or perhaps his family doing someting together. Reticent children may find it easier to talk through the medium of a glove puppet than directly to the interviewer. Anatomically correct dolls are most often provided for children aged 3 years or under, who can use them to demonstrate abuse, or to augment information revealed in drawings. As a general principle, the recall of events and their detail are greatly enhanced by the availability of play materials such as small dolls houses and human figures.

The child's mood throughout the interview should be monitored, taking note of whether he is happy, friendly, unconcerned, shy, frightened, apprehensive, tearful, miserable, or in a state of 'frozen watchfulness'. If negative emotions are expressed, the interviewer should acknowledge them and attempt to empathise. Frightened children often respond to encouragement to play freely. At the end of the interview, the child should be reassured and led to understand that the interviewer is aware of the difficult feelings with which he is struggling. The interviewer needs to provide an explicit acknowledgement of the importance of the session.

Chapter Ten

Psychological tests

There are a number of advantages in having available a small selection of psychological tests with which the interviewer has made himself familiar. On the simplest level they can be used as games or puzzles with which to engage the child's interest. They also act in a non-specific way as tests of the child's persistence and attention span, which are likely to be impaired in children with brain damage, neurosis or antisocial behaviour. Persistence and attention span are best estimated by giving the child a task to perform which is near the limit of his abilities and observing how rapidly he becomes frustrated and gives up.

The tests also yield more specific information about the child's level of intelligence, particular kinds of learning defects, organic impairment of cerebral function, and neurotic problems. Four psychological tests which cover a range of abilities and possible dysfunctions are described briefly below.

Bender gestalt

This consists of nine cards with a different design on each. The child is shown each card in turn and asked to copy the design. The cards are then removed and he is asked to reproduce the designs from memory. A manual that accompanies the test describes the kind of responses that indicate brain damage and those that are associated with a variety of neurotic disturbances. The second part of the test provides a way of assessing the intactness of short-term memory.

Goodenough draw-a-person test

The child is simply asked to make a drawing of a person. Standards are available for scoring the amount of detail included by the child, such as eyebrows and a definite neck. From these an approximate Intelligence Quotient can be readily calculated.

Peabody picture vocabulary test

A set of four pictures is shown and the child is given the name of one of them and asked to point to it. The test consists of a series of these sets, of increasing difficulty. As the child does not have to speak to score correctly, the test gives an indication of the extent of his passive vocabulary. The verbal Intelligence Quotient derived from this test is a good indication of the child's level of general intelligence.

Koh's block design

The child is given a number of blocks with various colours and patterns on their faces. He is shown a page with a design on it and asked to reproduce it by assembling the blocks in the correct way. The test comes with a booklet of designs of increasing difficulty. The number of designs the child can reproduce correctly gives a measure of his non-verbal Intelligence Quotient.

REFERENCE

JONES, D. P. H. & McQUISTON, M. G. (1988) *Interviewing the Sexually Abused Child.* Gaskell, London.

Case Presentation

The interviewer who has carefully gone through the foregoing scheme for history-taking and assessing the present mental state of a patient will have accumulated a great many facts. The ordering of these facts to present a coherent account of the patient's condition is not only essential for the purpose of examinations and ward rounds. It is also an excellent habit for the interviewer to acquire, as it enables him to think clearly about each patient and to come to a decision regarding the likely diagnosis which is firmly based on the available evidence. The issue of differential diagnosis is central, and the material should be organised on this basis. The information should be presented in such a way that the listener can appreciate the logical steps that narrow down the full range of possible diagnoses. This requires the interviewer to select from the mass of facts he has collected only those that are of immediate relevance. In this respect negative information may be every bit as important as positive information. For example, if the interviewer has made a provisional diagnosis of schizophrenia or manic-depressive psychosis and there is no family history of these conditions, he should mention the fact. This informs the listener that the interviewer is aware of the occurrence of familial cases in the functional psychoses and has taken care to inquire about them.

Facts that *conflict* with the interviewer's main provisional diagnosis should be particularly highlighted in the presentation. For instance, if the most likely diagnosis is schizophrenia, but there is a family history of manic-depressive psychosis, this should be mentioned with particular emphasis. However, the fact that it does not fit with the interviewer's presumed diagnosis should be reserved for his discussion of the differential diagnosis at the end of this presentation.

In his presentation, the interviewer should focus on the abnormal rather than the normal. It is unnecessary and tedious to present in meticulous detail facts about a *normal* childhood or schooling, for instance. It is sufficient to state that the patient's childhood and schooling were normal. This is a judgement which the clinician is expected to make and of which he should be capable. The abnormal findings should be presented in an orderly fashion, using the same scheme the interviewer has employed to organise his history-taking and mental state examination. It is helpful for the listener if the interviewer introduces each section of his findings with the appropriate heading. For example: 'In the *mental state* there was no abnormality of *behaviour*. The patient's *mood* was moderately depressed. In his *thought content* he exhibited ideas of self-blame and suicidal feelings.' If information from relatives or others has been obtained it should be brought in at the appropriate point either to supplement the patient's account or, occasionally, to contradict it.

As stressed earlier, the interviewer should record in detail the patient's exact words when they indicate the presence of important symptoms. However, it is unnecessary to go into this much detail when initially presenting abnormalities in the mental state. These should be given in a summary form, for example: 'The patient shows delusions of control, third person auditory hallucinations, derealisation and obsessional thoughts.' The interviewer should, of course, be prepared to furnish details of his own observations and the patient's exact statements if asked to do so, in order to support his assertion that a particular symptom is present.

Having presented the abnormal findings in a systematic way, the interviewer should then move on to the differential diagnosis. If he is confident that there is only one possible diagnosis, he should say so and provide the evidence for it. However, this is an unusual situation with psychiatric patients. More commonly there are two, three or even more alternative diagnoses. The interviewer should put these in order of likelihood and present the most likely diagnosis first. Having presented the differential diagnosis, he should then put forward the evidence for and against each possibility in turn, as concisely as possible. For example: 'The most likely diagnosis is schizophrenia. The patient exhibits paranoid delusions and delusions of reference of several months duration and there is a family history of schizophrenia. On the other hand, he is also significantly depressed and this could be viewed as a primary affective illness with a paranoid colouring from the patient's premorbid personality, which was solitary and suspicious.'

It is quite usual for more than one psychiatric condition to coexist in the same patient. In this event, the various conditions should not be presented as alternatives in the differential diagnosis. For example, the patient's personality may be abnormal as well as there being a frank psychiatric illness. The interviewer should present the psychiatric illness as the primary diagnosis and the personality abnormality as a subsidiary additional diagnosis. The possibility of an organic cause for psychiatric symptoms should also be borne in mind and included in the differential diagnosis where relevant. The kind of organic condition likely to give rise to the particular symptoms shown should be specified. Drug abuse should always be considered in this respect.

When discussing diagnosis, the interviewer should confine himself, as far as possible, to the categories laid down in the International Classification of Diseases. Although far from ideal, particularly in the area of personality abnormalities, this list provides a generally accepted categorisation which makes communication between psychiatric professionals easier. If a particular kind of abnormal personality is cited as part of the differential diagnosis, the interviewer must be ready to support it with good evidence from the patient's past behaviour and usual temperament. The categories of personality abnormality are particularly elastic and hence are often used in a sloppy way.

Following the presentation and discussion of differential diagnosis, the interviewer should specify the additional information required in order to decide on a firm diagnosis. This may be

139

additional history from other informants, further observation of the patient, or psychological and laboratory tests. The response to treatment should be proposed as a way of determining the diagnosis *only as a last resort.*

The interviewer should then discuss possible causes of the patient's condition, including a formulation of the psycho-dynamics where appropriate, and possible methods of treatment, and should make an assessment of the prognosis. These issues are outside the scope of this book.

WRITTEN FORMULATION

It is always useful for the interviewer, for his own sake and for the sake of other people who need to look through the case-notes, to provide a written formulation of the case once the initial assessment is complete. This should comprise a short summary of the topics discussed above. They need to be presented in an orderly way, preferably under headings, so that the formulation can be read quickly and easily.

When a formulation is being written for the purposes of a clinical examination, brevity and clarity are of the greatest importance. It is advisable to use underlined headings and to include the relevant information under each heading in note form. An example of this approach follows.

Patient: Englishman age 22.

Family History: Maternal aunt has schizophrenia.

Personal History: Normal childhood and schooling. No O-levels or A-levels.

Occupations: Poor work record. 15 jobs in 7 years.

Sexual History: Never any steady girlfriend.

Past Illnesses: Nil.

Premorbid Personality: No close friends. Sensitive. Has abused drugs and alcohol in past.

Symptoms: History of auditory and visual hallucinations for 2 weeks.

On Examination: Behaviour: Tense and restless.
Mood: Anxious and suspicious.
Speech: 1. Form: Normal.
2. Content: Paranoid delusions.
Grandiose delusions.
Third person auditory hallucinations.
Depersonalisation.

Differential diagnosis:

1. Primary diagnosis: Schizophrenia.
   Subsidiary diagnosis: Schizoid personality.
2. Drug induced psychosis. ?LSD. ?Amphetamines.

Investigations: Urine for amphetamines.
Keep off all medication and observe.

Treatment: If no improvement off drugs, start phenothiazines.

Index

Index

Index